Microsoft® Office Excel 2003

ILLUSTRATED

ADVANCED

Microsoft® Office Specialist
Approved Courseware

(3 of 3)

Lynn Wermers

THOMSON
COURSE TECHNOLOGY

Australia • Canada • Mexico • Singapore • Spain • United Kingdom • United States

MW00355093

Microsoft® Office Excel 2003 - Illustrated Advanced

Lynn Wermers

Executive Editor:
Nicole Jones Pinard

Product Managers:
Christina Kling Garrett,
Jane Hosie-Bounar,
Jeanne Herring

Associate Product Manager:
Emilie Perreault

Production Editor:
Aimee Poirier

Developmental Editor:
Barbara Clemens

Editorial Assistant:
Abbey Reider

QA Manuscript Reviewers:
Alex White, Chris Carvalho

Composition House:
GEX Publishing Services

Text Designer:
Joseph Lee, Black Fish Design

COPYRIGHT © 2004 Course Technology, a division of Thomson Learning™. Thomson Learning™ is a trademark used herein under license.

Printed in the United States of America

2 3 4 5 6 7 8 9 BM 08 07 06 05

For more information, contact Course Technology, 25 Thomson Place, Boston, Massachusetts, 02210.

Or you can visit us on the World Wide Web at www.course.com

ALL RIGHTS RESERVED. No part of this work covered by the copyright hereon may be reproduced or used in any form or by any means—graphic, electronic, or mechanical, including photocopying, recording, taping, Web distribution, or information storage and retrieval systems—without the written permission of the publisher.

For permission to use material from this text or product, submit a request online at www.thomsonrights.com. Any additional questions about permissions can be submitted by e-mail to thomsonrights@thomson.com.

Trademarks
Some of the product names and company names used in this book have been used for identification purposes only and may be trademarks or registered trademarks of their respective manufacturers and sellers.

Microsoft and the Office logo are either registered trademarks or trademarks of Microsoft Corporation in the United States and/or other countries. Course Technology is an independent entity from Microsoft Corporation, and not affiliated with Microsoft in any manner.

This text may be used in assisting students to prepare for a Microsoft Office Specialist Exam. Neither Microsoft Corporation, its designated review company, nor Course Technology warrants that use of this text will ensure passing the relevant exam.

Use of the Microsoft Office Specialist Approved Courseware Logo on this product signifies that it has been independently reviewed and approved in complying with the following standards: "Includes acceptable coverage of all content related to the Microsoft Office Exam entitled Microsoft Office Excel 2003 and sufficient performance-based exercises that relate closely to all required content, based on sampling of text."

ISBN 0-619-05774-2

The Illustrated Series Vision

Teaching and writing about computer applications can be extremely rewarding and challenging. How do we engage students and keep their interest? How do we teach them skills that they can easily apply on the job? As we set out to write this book, our goals were to develop a textbook that:

- works for a beginning student
- provides varied, flexible, and meaningful exercises and projects to reinforce the skills
- serves as a reference tool
- makes your job as an educator easier, by providing resources above and beyond the textbook to help you teach your course

Our popular, streamlined format is based on advice from instructional designers and customers. This flexible design presents each lesson on a two-page spread, with step-by-step instructions on the left, and screen illustrations on the right. This signature style, coupled with high-caliber content, provides a comprehensive yet manageable introduction to Microsoft Office Excel 2003—it is a teaching package for the instructor and a learning experience for the student.

Acknowledgments

I would like to thank Barbara Clemens for her insightful contributions and guidance. I would also like to thank Christina Kling Garrett for patiently answering and researching my endless questions.

Lynn Wermers

Preface

Welcome to *Microsoft Office® Excel 2003– Illustrated Advanced*. Each lesson in this book contains elements pictured to the right.

How is the book organized?

The book is organized into five units on Excel, covering what-if analysis, PivotTables and PivotCharts, exchanging data with other programs, customizing Excel, and programming with Excel.

What kinds of assignments are included in the book? At what level of difficulty?

The lessons use MediaLoft, a fictional chain of bookstores, as the case study. The assignments on the light purple pages at the end of each unit increase in difficulty. Data files and case studies, with many international examples, provide a great variety of interesting and relevant business applications. Assignments include:

- **Concepts Reviews** include multiple choice, matching, and screen identification questions.

- **Skills Reviews** provide additional hands-on, step-by-step reinforcement.

- **Independent Challenges** are case projects requiring critical thinking and application of the unit skills. The Independent Challenges increase in difficulty, with the first one in each unit being the easiest (most step-by-step with detailed instructions). Independent Challenges 2 and 3 become increasingly open-ended, requiring more independent problem solving.

- **E-Quest Independent Challenges** are case projects with a Web focus. E-Quests require the use of the World Wide Web to conduct research to complete the project.

- **Advanced Challenge Exercises** set within the Independent Challenges provide optional steps for more advanced students.

- **Visual Workshops** are practical, self-graded capstone projects that require independent problem solving.

Each 2-page spread focuses on a single skill.

Concise text introduces the basic principles in the lesson and integrates a real-world case study.

UNIT
L
Excel 2003

Changing the Summary Function of a PivotTable Report

A PivotTable's **summary function** controls how Excel calculates the table data. Unless you specify otherwise, Excel applies the SUM function to numeric data and the COUNT function to data fields containing text. However, you can easily change the SUM function to a different summary function, such as AVERAGE, which calculates the average of all values in the field. Jim wants you to calculate the average sales for the northeastern cities using the AVERAGE function.

STEPS

1. **Click any cell in the data area (A3:I20), then click the** Field Settings button **on the PivotTable toolbar**
   The PivotTable toolbar buttons are described in Table L-1. The PivotTable Field dialog box opens. The selected function in the Summarize by list box determines how the data is calculated.

2. **In the Summarize by list box, click** Average, **then click** OK
   The PivotTable Field dialog box closes. The data area of the PivotTable shows the average sales for each product by city and quarter. See Figure L-6. After reviewing the data, you decide that it would be more useful to sum the salary information than to average it.

QUICK TIP
When you name a PivotTable sheet, it is best to avoid using spaces in the name. If a PivotTable name contains a space, you must put single quotes around the name when you refer to it in a function.

3. **Click** 📊 **on the PivotTable toolbar; in the Summarize by list box, click** Sum, **then click** OK
   The PivotTable Field dialog box closes and Excel recalculates the PivotTable—this time, summing the sales data instead of averaging it.

4. **Rename Sheet1** PivotTable, **add your name to the worksheet footer, then save the workbook and print the worksheet in landscape orientation.**

TABLE L-1: PivotTable toolbar buttons

button	name	description
PivotTable ▾	PivotTable Menu	Displays menu of PivotTable commands
	Format Report	Displays a list of PivotTable AutoFormats
	Chart Wizard	Creates a PivotChart report
	Hide Detail	Hides detail in table groupings
	Show Detail	Shows detail in table groupings
	Refresh Data	Updates list changes within the table
	Include Hidden Items in Totals	Includes values for all items in totals, including hidden items
	Always Display Items	Turns on drop-down selections for PivotTable fields
	Field Settings	Displays a list of field settings
	Show/Hide Field List	Displays/hides PivotTable Field List window; in a chart, displays or hides outlines and labels

EXCEL L-6 ANALYZING DATA WITH PIVOTTABLES

Tips, as well as troubleshooting advice, right where you need them—next to the step itself.

Tables provide quickly accessible summaries of key terms, toolbar buttons, or keyboard alternatives connected with the lesson material. Students can refer easily to this information when working on their own projects at a later time.

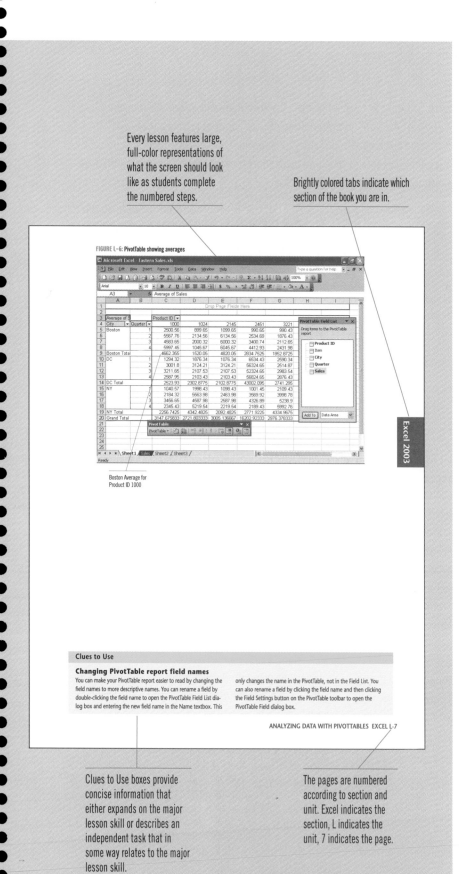

Every lesson features large, full-color representations of what the screen should look like as students complete the numbered steps.

Brightly colored tabs indicate which section of the book you are in.

FIGURE L-6: PivotTable showing averages

Boston Average for Product ID 1000

Excel 2003

Clues to Use

Changing PivotTable report field names

You can make your PivotTable report easier to read by changing the field names to more descriptive names. You can rename a field by double-clicking the field name to open the PivotTable Field List dialog box and entering the new field name in the Name textbox. This only changes the name in the PivotTable, not in the Field List. You can also rename a field by clicking the field name and then clicking the Field Settings button on the PivotTable toolbar to open the PivotTable Field dialog box.

ANALYZING DATA WITH PIVOTTABLES EXCEL L-7

Clues to Use boxes provide concise information that either expands on the major lesson skill or describes an independent task that in some way relates to the major lesson skill.

The pages are numbered according to section and unit. Excel indicates the section, L indicates the unit, 7 indicates the page.

What online content solutions are available to accompany this book?

Visit www.course.com for more information on our online content for Illustrated titles. Options include:

MyCourse 2.0

Need a quick, simple tool to help you manage your course? Try MyCourse 2.0, the easiest to use, most flexible syllabus and content management tool available. MyCourse 2.0 offers you brand new content, including Topic Reviews, Extra Case Projects, and Quizzes, to accompany this book.

WebCT

Course Technology and WebCT have partnered to provide you with the highest quality online resources and Web-based tools for your class. Course Technology offers content for this book to help you create your WebCT class, such as a suggested Syllabus, Lecture Notes, Practice Test questions, and more.

Blackboard

Course Technology and Blackboard have also partnered to provide you with the highest quality online resources and Web-based tools for your class. Course Technology offers content for this book to help you create your Blackboard class, such as a suggested Syllabus, Lecture Notes, Practice Test questions, and more.

Is this book Microsoft Office Specialist Certified?

When used in conjunction with *Microsoft Office Excel 2003 – Illustrated Basic* and *Microsoft Office Excel 2003 – Illustrated Intermediate,* this book covers the objectives for Microsoft Office Excel 2003 and Microsoft Office Excel 2003 Expert. When used in this sequence, these titles have received certification approval as courseware for the Microsoft Office Specialist program. See the inside front cover for more information on other Illustrated titles meeting Microsoft Office Specialist certification.

The first page of each unit indicates which objectives in the unit are Microsoft Office Specialist skills. If an objective is set in red, it meets a Microsoft Office Specialist skill. A document on the CD accompanying this book cross-references the skills with the lessons and exercises.

Instructor Resources

The Instructor Resources CD is Course Technology's way of putting the resources and information needed to teach and learn effectively into your hands. With an integrated array of teaching and learning tools that offers you and your students a broad range of technology-based instructional options, we believe this CD represents the highest quality and most cutting edge resources available to instructors today. Many of these resources are available at www.course.com. The resources available with this book are:

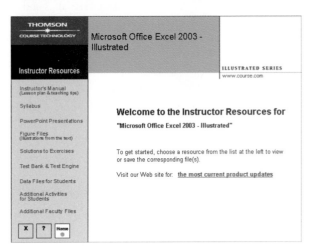

- **Data Files for Students**—To complete most of the units in this book, your students will need the **Data Files** on the CD in the back of this book. The Data Files are also available on the Instructor Resources CD and can be downloaded from www.course.com.

  Instruct students to use the **Data Files List** located on the CD. This list gives instructions on copying and organizing files.

- **Solutions to Exercises**—Solutions to Exercises contains every file students are asked to create or modify in the lessons and End-of-Unit material. A Help file on the Instructor Resources CD includes information for using the Solution Files. There is also a document outlining the solutions for the End-of-Unit Concepts Review, Skills Review, and Independent Challenges.

- PowerPoint Presentations—Each unit has a corresponding PowerPoint presentation that you can use in a lecture, distribute to your students, or customize to suit your course.

- **Instructor's Manual**—Available as an electronic file, the Instructor's Manual is quality-assurance tested and includes unit overviews, and detailed lecture topics with teaching tips for each unit.

- Sample Syllabus—Prepare and customize your course easily using this sample course outline.

- Figure Files—The figures in the text are provided on the Instructor Resources CD to help you illustrate key topics or concepts. You can create traditional overhead transparencies by printing the figure files. Or you can create electronic slide shows by using the figures in a presentation program such as PowerPoint.

- ExamView—ExamView is a powerful testing software package that allows you to create and administer printed, computer (LAN-based), and Internet exams. ExamView includes hundreds of questions that correspond to the topics covered in this text, enabling students to generate detailed study guides that include page references for further review. The computer-based and Internet testing components allow students to take exams at their computers, and also saves you time by grading each exam automatically.

SAM 2003 Assessment & Training

SAM 2003 helps you energize your class exams and training assignments by allowing students to learn and test important computer skills in an active, hands-on environment.

With SAM 2003 Assessment, you create powerful interactive exams on critical applications such as Word, Outlook, PowerPoint, Windows, the Internet, and much more. The exams simulate the application environment, allowing your students to demonstrate their knowledge and think through the skills by performing real-world tasks.

Designed to be used with the Illustrated series, SAM 2003 Assessment & Training includes built-in page references so students can create study guides that match the Illustrated textbooks you use in class. Powerful administrative options allow you to schedule exams and assignments, secure your tests, and run reports with almost limitless flexibility.

Contents

Read This Before You Begin

Software Information and Required Installation

This book was written and tested using Microsoft Office 2003 - Professional Edition, with a typical installation on Microsoft Windows XP plus installation of the latest Service Pack, and with Internet Explorer 6.0 or higher. Some of the exercises in this book assume that your computer is connected to the Internet. If you are not connected to the Internet, see your instructor for information.

Tips for Students

What are Data Files?

To complete many of the units in this book, you need to use Data Files from the CD in the back of this book. A Data File contains a partially completed document, so that you don't have to type in all the information in the document yourself. Your instructor can give you instructions on how to organize your files, as well as a complete file listing, or you can find the list and the instructions for organizing your files on the CD.

Why is my screen different from the book?

Your Desktop components and some dialog box options might be different if you are using an operating system other than Windows XP.

Depending on your computer hardware and the display settings on your computer, you may also notice the following differences:

- Your screen may look larger or smaller because of your screen resolution (the height and width of your screen).

- Your title bars and dialog boxes may not display file extensions. To display file extensions, click Start on the taskbar, click Control Panel, click Appearance and Themes, then click Folder Options. Click the View tab if necessary, click Hide extensions for known file types to deselect it, then click OK. Your Office dialog boxes and title bars should now display file extensions.

- The colors of the title bar in your screen may be a solid blue, and the cells in Excel may appear different from the orange and gray because of your color settings

- Depending on your Office settings, your toolbars may be displayed on a single row and your menus may display a shortened list of frequently used commands. Office menus and toolbars can modify themselves to your working style by displaying only the most frequently used buttons and menu commands. To view buttons not currently displayed, click a Toolbar Options button ⁝ at the end of either the Standard or Formatting toolbar. To view the full list of menu commands, click the double arrow at the bottom of the menu.

Toolbars in one row

Toolbars in two rows

In order to have your toolbars displayed in two rows, showing all buttons, and to have the full menus displayed, you must turn off the personalized menus and toolbars feature. Click Tools on the menu bar, click Customize, select the show Standard and Formatting toolbars on two rows and Always show full menus check boxes on the Options tab, and then click Close. This book assumes you are displaying toolbars in two rows and displaying full menus.

Using What-if Analysis

OBJECTIVES

Define a what-if analysis

Track a what-if analysis with Scenario Manager

Generate a scenario summary

Project figures using a data table

Create a two-input data table

Use Goal Seek

Set up a complex what-if analysis with Solver

Run Solver and generate an Answer Report

If you have a SAM user profile, you may have access to hands-on instruction, practice, and assessment of the skills covered in this unit. Log in to your SAM account and go to your assignments page to see what your instructor has assigned.

Each time you use a worksheet to explore different outcomes for Excel formulas, you are performing a **what-if analysis**. For example, what would happen to a firm's overall expense budget if company travel expenses decreased by 30%? Using Excel, you can perform a what-if analysis in many ways. In this unit, you will learn to track what-if scenarios and generate summary reports using the Excel Scenario Manager. You will design and manipulate one-input and two-input data tables to project multiple outcomes. Also, you will use the Goal Seek feature to solve a what-if analysis. Finally, you will use Solver to perform a complex what-if analysis involving multiple variables. The MediaLoft corporate office is considering the purchase of several pieces of capital equipment, as well as several vehicles. They have asked you to help analyze their options using Excel.

UNIT K
Excel 2003

Defining a What-if Analysis

By performing a what-if analysis in a worksheet, you can get immediate answers to questions such as "What happens to profits if we sell 30% more of a certain product?" or "What happens to monthly payments if interest rates rise or fall?" A worksheet you use to produce a what-if analysis is often called a **model** because it acts as the basis for multiple outcomes. To perform a what-if analysis in a worksheet, you change the value in one or more **input cells** (cells that contain data rather than formulas), then observe the effects on dependent cells. A **dependent cell** usually contains a formula whose resulting value changes depending on the values in the input cells. A dependent cell can be located either in the same worksheet as the changing input value or in another worksheet. ▰▰▰▰ Jim Fernandez has created a worksheet model to perform an initial what-if analysis of equipment loan payments. See Figure K-1. You will follow the guidelines below to perform a what-if analysis for him.

DETAILS

- **Understand and state the purpose of the worksheet model**
  The worksheet model is designed to calculate a fixed-rate, monthly equipment loan payment.

- **Determine the data input value(s) that, if changed, affect the dependent cell results**
  The model contains three data input values (labeled Loan Amount, Annual Interest Rate, and Term in Months), in cells B4, B5, and B6, respectively.

- **Identify the dependent cell(s), usually containing formulas, that will contain adjusted results as different data values are entered**
  There are three dependent cell formulas (labeled Monthly Payment, Total Payments, and Total Interest). The results appear in cells B9, B10, and B11, respectively.

- **Formulate questions you want the what-if analysis to answer**
  You want to answer the following questions with this model: (1) What happens to the monthly payments if the interest rate is 7%? (2) What happens to the monthly payments if the loan term is 60 months (five years) instead of 48 months (four years)? (3) What happens to the monthly payments if less-expensive equipment is purchased with a lower loan amount?

- **Perform the what-if analysis and explore the relationships between the input values and the dependent cell formulas**
  You want to see what effect a 7% interest rate has on the dependent cell formulas. Because the interest rate is located in cell B5, any formula that references cell B5 is directly affected by a change in interest rate—in this case, the Monthly Payment formula in cell B9. Because the formula in cell B10 references cell B9 and the formula in cell B11 references cell B10, however, a change in the interest rate in cell B5 affects these other two formulas as well. Figure K-2 shows the result of the what-if analysis described in this example.

FIGURE K-1: Worksheet model for a what-if analysis

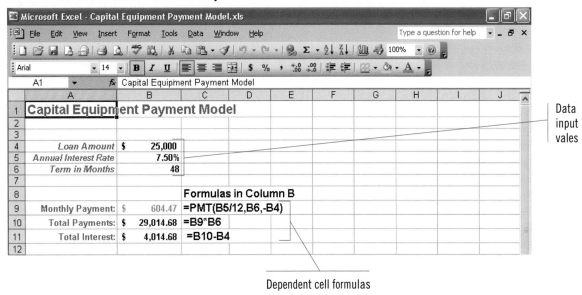

Data input vales

Dependent cell formulas

Excel 2003

FIGURE K-2: What-if analysis with changed input value and dependent formula results

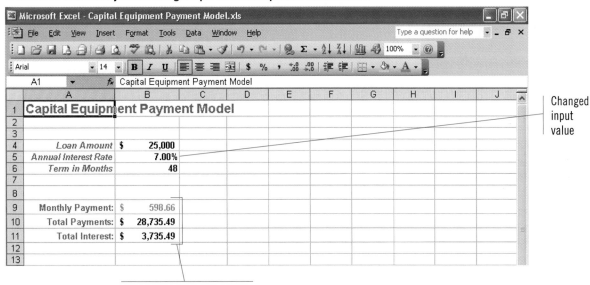

Changed input value

Dependent cell values affected by changed input value

Tracking a What-if Analysis with Scenario Manager

A **scenario** is a set of values you use to forecast worksheet results. The Excel Scenario Manager simplifies the process of what-if analysis by allowing you to name and save different scenarios with the worksheet. Scenarios are particularly useful when you work with uncertain or changing variables. If you plan to create a budget, for example, but are uncertain of your revenue, you can assign several different revenue values, then switch between the scenarios to perform a what-if analysis of the effects of each revenue figure on profits.  Jim asks you to use Scenario Manager to consider three equipment loan scenarios: (1) the original loan quote, (2) a longer-term loan, and (3) a reduced loan amount.

STEPS

1. **Start Excel, open the Data File** EX K-1.xls **from the drive and folder where your Data Files are stored, then save it as** Capital Equipment Payment Model

   The first step in defining a scenario is choosing the cells that will vary in the different scenarios; these are known as **changing cells**.

2. **On the Single Loan sheet, select range B4:B6, click** Tools **on the menu bar, then click** Scenarios

   The Scenario Manager dialog box opens with the following message: "No Scenarios defined. Choose Add to add scenarios."

3. **Click** Add, **drag the Add Scenario dialog box to the right if necessary until columns A and B are visible, then type** Original loan quote **in the Scenario name text box**

   The range in the Changing cells box reflects your initial selection, as shown in Figure K-3.

4. **Click** OK **to confirm the Add Scenario settings**

   The Scenario Values dialog box opens, as shown in Figure K-4. The existing values appear in the changing cell boxes. Because this first scenario reflects the original loan quote input values ($25,000 at 7.5% for 48 months), these values are correct.

5. **Click** OK

   The Scenario Manager dialog box reappears with the new scenario listed in the Scenarios box. You want to create a second scenario, this one with a loan term of 60 months.

QUICK TIP
You can delete a scenario by selecting it in the Scenario Manager dialog box and clicking Delete.

6. **Click** Add; **in the Scenario name text box type** Longer term loan, **click** OK; **in the Scenario Values dialog box, select** 48 **in the third changing cell box, type** 60, **then click** Add

   You also want to consider a scenario that uses $21,000 as the loan amount.

7. **In the Scenario name text box, type** Reduced loan amount, **click** OK; **in the Scenario Values dialog box, change the** 25000 **in the first changing cell box to** 21000, **then click** OK

   The Scenario Manager dialog box reappears. See Figure K-5. All three scenarios are listed, with the most recent—Reduced loan amount—selected. Now that you have defined the three scenarios, you want to apply them and see what effect they have on the monthly payment.

8. **Make sure the Reduced loan amount scenario is still selected, click** Show, **notice that the monthly payment in the worksheet changes from $604.47 to $507.76; click** Longer term loan, **click** Show, **notice that the monthly payment is now $500.95; click** Original loan quote, **click** Show **to return to the original values, then click** Close

9. **Save the workbook**

FIGURE K-3: Add Scenario dialog box

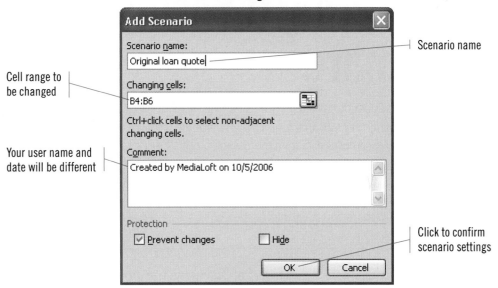

Scenario name →

Cell range to be changed →

Your user name and date will be different →

Click to confirm scenario settings

FIGURE K-4: Scenario Values dialog box

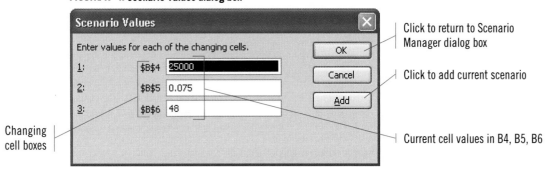

Click to return to Scenario Manager dialog box

Click to add current scenario

Changing cell boxes

Current cell values in B4, B5, B6

FIGURE K-5: Scenario Manager dialog box with three scenarios listed

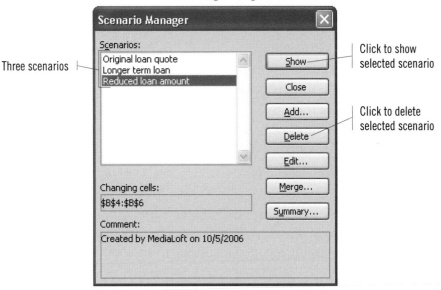

Three scenarios

Click to show selected scenario

Click to delete selected scenario

Clues to Use

Merging scenarios

To bring scenarios from another workbook into the current workbook, click the Merge button in the Scenario Manager dialog box. The Merge Scenarios dialog box opens, letting you select scenarios from other workbooks.

Generating a Scenario Summary

Although it may be useful to switch between different scenarios when analyzing data, in most cases you will want to refer to a single report summarizing the results of the scenarios in a worksheet. A **scenario summary** is an Excel table that compiles data from the changing cells and corresponding result cells for each scenario. You can use a scenario summary to illustrate the best, worst, and most likely scenarios for a particular set of circumstances. Naming the cells makes the summary easier to read because the names, not the cell references, appear in the report. ████ Now that you have defined Jim's scenarios, he needs you to generate and print a scenario summary report. You begin by creating cell names in column B based on the labels in column A.

STEPS

QUICK TIP
To delete a range name, click Insert on the menu bar, point to Name, click Define, click the range name, then click Delete.

1. **Select the range A4:B11, click Insert on the menu bar, point to Name, click Create, click the Left column check box to select it if necessary, then click OK**
   Excel creates the names based on the labels in column A.

2. **Click cell B4 to make sure Loan_Amount appears in the Name box, then click the Name Box list arrow**
   All six labels appear in the Name Box list, confirming that they were created. See Figure K-6. Now you are ready to generate the scenario summary report.

3. **Press [Esc] to close the Name Box list, click Tools on the menu bar, click Scenarios, then click Summary in the Scenario Manager dialog box**
   The Scenario Summary dialog box opens. Scenario summary is selected, indicating that it is the default report type. Excel needs to know the location of the cells that contain the formula results.

4. **Select the Result cells box, if necessary, then select range B9:B11 in the worksheet**
   With the report type and result cells specified, as shown in Figure K-7, you are now ready to generate the report.

QUICK TIP
The scenario summary is not linked to the worksheet. If you change the cells in the worksheet, you must generate a new scenario summary.

5. **Click OK**
   The summary of the worksheet's scenarios appears on a new sheet titled Scenario Summary. The report appears in outline format so that you can hide or show report details. Because the Current Values column shows the same values as the Original loan quote column, you decide to delete column D.

6. **Right-click the column D heading, then click Delete in the shortcut menu**
   The column containing the current values is deleted, and the Original loan quote column data shifts to the left. Next, you want to delete the notes at the bottom of the report because they refer to the column that no longer exists. You also want to make the report title more descriptive.

7. **Select the range B13:B15, press [Delete], select cell B2, edit its contents to read Scenario Summary for Equipment Loan, then click cell A1**
   The completed scenario summary is shown in Figure K-8.

8. **Add your name to the left section of the Summary sheet footer, save the workbook, then preview and print the report in landscape orientation**

Name Box list arrow

Names match labels in column A

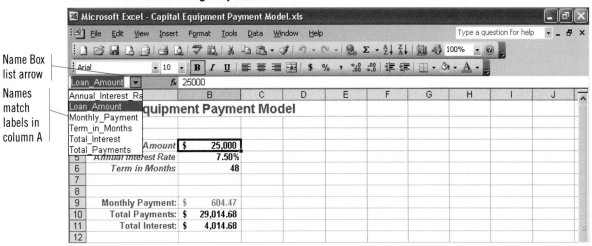

Default report type

Cells to be recalculated when a new scenario is applied

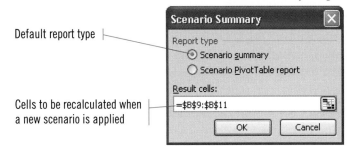

Column D now contains original loan quote

Report is in outline format

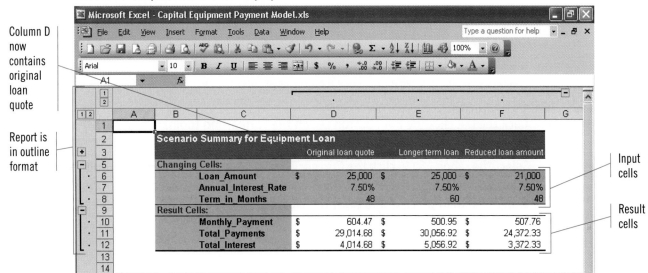

Input cells

Result cells

Excel 2003

Projecting Figures Using a Data Table

Another way to answer what-if questions in a worksheet is by using a data table. A **data table** is a range of cells that shows the resulting values when one or more input values is varied in a formula. For example, you could use a data table to calculate your monthly mortgage payment based on several different interest rates simultaneously. A **one-input data table** is a table that shows the result of varying one input value, such as the interest rate. ▰▰▰▰ Now that you have completed Jim's analysis, he wants you to find out how the monthly equipment payments would change as interest rates increased by increments of 0.25%. He estimates that the lowest interest rate would be about 7.00% and the highest 8.00%. You begin by creating a table structure, with the varying interest rates listed in the left column.

STEPS

1. **Click the Single Loan sheet tab, select cell D4, type Interest, select cell D5, type 7.00%, select cell D6, type 7.25%; select the range D5:D6, drag the fill handle to select the range D7:D9, then release the mouse button**

   With the varying interest rates (input values) listed in column D, you need to enter a formula reference to cell B9. This tells Excel to use the formula in cell B9 to calculate multiple results in column E, based on the changing interest rates in column D.

2. **Click cell E4, type =B9, then click the Enter button ✓ on the Formula bar**

   The value in cell B9, $604.47, now appears in cell E4, and the formula reference (=B9) appears in the formula bar. See Figure K-9. Because the value in cell E4 isn't a part of the data table (Excel only uses it to calculate the values in the table), you want to hide the contents of cell E4 from view.

3. **With cell E4 selected, click Format on the menu bar, click Cells, click the Number tab in the Format Cells dialog box if necessary, click Custom under Category, delete the codes in the Type box, type ;;; in the Type box, then click OK**

   The three semicolons hide the values in a cell. With the table structure in place, you can now generate the data table showing monthly payment values for the varying interest rates.

TROUBLE
If you receive the message "Selection not valid," repeat Step 4, taking care to select the entire range D4:E9.

4. **Select range D4:E9, click Data on the menu bar, then click Table**

   You have highlighted the range that makes up the table structure. The Table dialog box opens, as shown in Figure K-10. This is where you indicate in which worksheet cell you want the varying input values (the interest rates in column D) to be substituted. Because the monthly payments formula in cell B9 (which you just referenced in cell E4) uses the annual interest rate in cell B5 as input, you enter a reference to cell B5. You place this reference in the Column input cell text box, rather than in the Row input cell text box, because the varying input values are arranged in a column in your data table structure.

QUICK TIP
You cannot delete individual values in a data table; you must clear all values.

5. **Click the Column input cell text box, click cell B5, then click OK**

   Excel generates the data table containing monthly payments for each interest rate. The monthly payment values appear next to the interest rates in column E. The new data and the heading in cell D4 need formatting.

6. **Click cell D4, click the Bold button B on the Formatting toolbar, then click the Align Right button ≣ on the Formatting toolbar**

7. **Select the range E5:E9, click the Currency Style button $ on the Formatting toolbar, select cell A1, add your name to the left section of the worksheet footer, save the workbook, then preview and print the worksheet**

   The completed data table appears as shown in Figure K-11. Notice that the monthly payment amount for a 7.50% interest rate is the same as the original loan quote in cell B9. You can use this information to cross-check the values that Excel generates in data tables.

FIGURE K-9: One-input data table structure

Reference to formula in cell D9

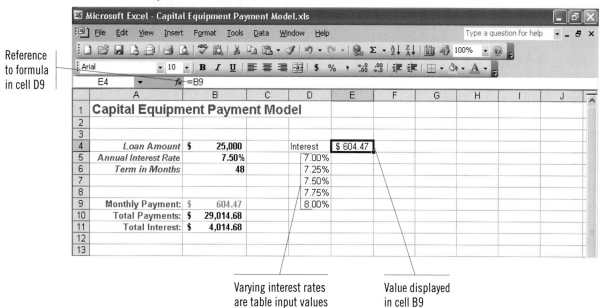

Varying interest rates are table input values

Value displayed in cell B9

FIGURE K-10: Table dialog box

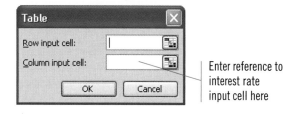

Enter reference to interest rate input cell here

FIGURE K-11: Completed data table with resulting values

Formatted heading

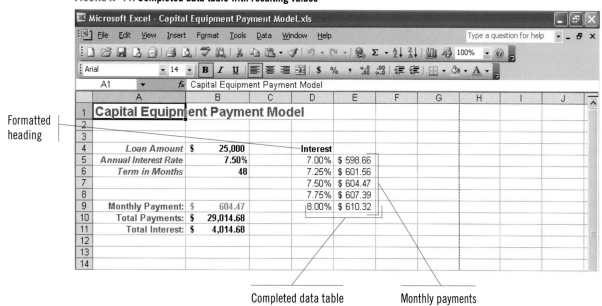

Completed data table

Monthly payments

Creating a Two-input Data Table

A **two-input data table** shows the resulting values when two different input values are varied in a formula. You could, for example, use a two-input data table to calculate your monthly mortgage payment based on varying interest rates and varying loan terms. In a two-input data table, different values of one input cell appear across the top row of the table, while different values of the second input cell are listed down the left column of the table. ▰▰▰▰ Jim wants you to use a two-input data table to see what happens if the various interest rates are applied across several different loan terms, such as three, four, and five years. You begin by changing the structure of the one-input data table to accommodate a two-input data table.

STEPS

1. **With the Single Loan sheet activated, move the contents of cell D4 to cell C7; click cell C8, type Rates, click the Enter button ✓ on the Formula bar, click the Align Right button ▤ on the Formatting toolbar, then click the Bold button B on the Formatting toolbar**
   The left table heading is in place. You don't need the old data table values, and it is best to clear the cell formatting when you delete the old values.

2. **Select the range E4:E9, click Edit on the menu bar, point to Clear, then click All**
   Labels for the two types of input can make the table easier to read.

   TROUBLE
   If you do not see the value you entered in cell E4, make sure you cleared both values and formats in the correct range in Step 2.

3. **Click cell F3, type Months, click ✓, click B, click cell E4, type 36, click ✓, click cell F4, type 48, click cell G4, type 60, then click ✓**
   With both top row and left column values and headings in place, you are ready to reference the monthly payment formula. This is the formula Excel uses to calculate the values in the table. Because it is not part of the table (Excel uses it only to calculate the values in the table), it is best to hide the cell contents from view.

4. **Click cell D4, type =B9, click ✓, click Format on the menu bar, click Cells, in the Format Cells dialog box click the Number tab if necessary, click Custom, delete the codes in the Type box, type ;;; in the Type box, then click OK**
   The two-input data table structure is complete, as shown in Figure K-12. You are ready to have Excel calculate the table values.

5. **Select the range D4:G9, click Data on the menu bar, then click Table**
   The Table dialog box opens. The loan terms are arranged in a row, so you enter a reference to the loan term input cell (B6) in the Row input cell text box. The interest rates are arranged in a column, so you enter a reference to the interest rate input cell (B5) in the Column input cell text box.

   TROUBLE
   If the Table dialog box obstructs your view of the worksheet, drag it out of the way.

6. **With the insertion point positioned in the Row input cell text box, click cell B6 in the worksheet, click the Column input cell text box, then click cell B5**
   See Figure K-13. The row input cell (B6) references the loan term, and the column input cell (B5) references the interest rate. Now, you can generate the data table values and format the results.

7. **Click OK, select the range E5:G9, click the Currency Style button $ on the Formatting toolbar, then click cell F7**
   The resulting values appear, as shown in Figure K-14. The value in cell F7 matches the original quote: a monthly payment of $604.47 for a 48-month loan of $25,000 at a 7.50% interest rate.

8. **Save the workbook, then preview and print the worksheet**

FIGURE K-12: Two-input data table structure

Formula reference

Table headings

Varying input values

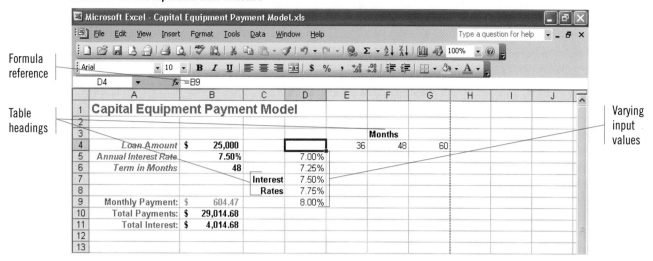

FIGURE K-13: Table dialog box

Loan term input cell

Interest rate input cell

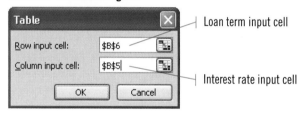

FIGURE K-14: Completed two-input data table

Hidden reference to cell B9

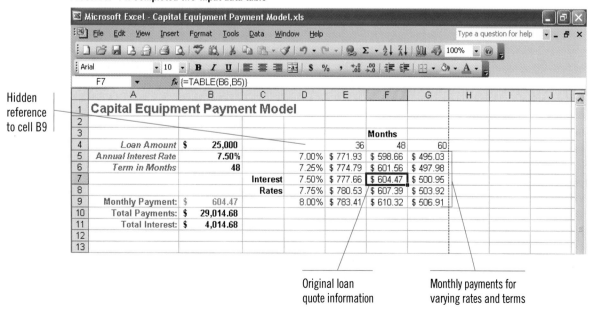

Original loan quote information

Monthly payments for varying rates and terms

Using Goal Seek

You can think of goal seeking as a what-if analysis in reverse. In a what-if analysis, you might try many sets of values to achieve a certain solution. To **goal seek**, you specify a solution, then find the input value that produces the answer you want. "Backing into" a solution in this way, sometimes referred to as **backsolving**, can save a significant amount of time. For example, you can use Goal Seek to determine how many units must be sold to reach a particular sales goal or to determine the expenses that must be cut to meet a budget. After reviewing his data table, Jim has a follow-up question: how much money could MediaLoft borrow if the company wanted to keep the total payment amount of all the equipment to $28,000? You use Goal Seek to answer his question.

STEPS

1. **On the Single Loan worksheet, click cell B10**

   The first step in using Goal Seek is to select a goal cell. A **goal cell** contains a formula in which you can substitute values to find a specific value, or goal. You use cell B10 as the goal cell because it contains the formula for total payments.

2. **Click Tools on the menu bar, then click Goal Seek**

   The Goal Seek dialog box opens. The Set cell box contains a reference to cell B10, the Total Payments cell you selected in Step 1. You need to indicate that the figure in cell B10 should not exceed 28000.

3. **Click the To value text box, then type 28000**

   The 28000 figure represents the desired solution you want to reach by substituting different values in the goal cell.

4. **Click the By changing cell box, then click cell B4**

   You have specified that you want cell B4, the loan amount, to change to reach the 28000 solution. See Figure K-15.

   QUICK TIP
   Before you select another command, you can return the worksheet to its status prior to the Goal Seek by pressing [Ctrl][Z].

5. **Click OK, then move the dialog box as necessary so that column B is visible**

   The Goal Seek Status dialog box opens with the following message: "Goal Seeking with Cell B10 found a solution." By changing the Loan Amount figure in cell B4 from $25,000 to $24,126, Goal Seek achieves a Total Payments goal of $28,000.

6. **Click OK**

   Changing the loan amount value in cell B4 changes all the values in the worksheet, including the data table. See Figure K-16.

7. **Save the workbook, then preview and print the worksheet**

FIGURE K-15: Completed Goal Seek dialog box

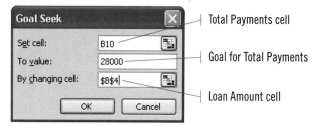

- Total Payments cell
- Goal for Total Payments
- Loan Amount cell

FIGURE K-16: Worksheet with new values

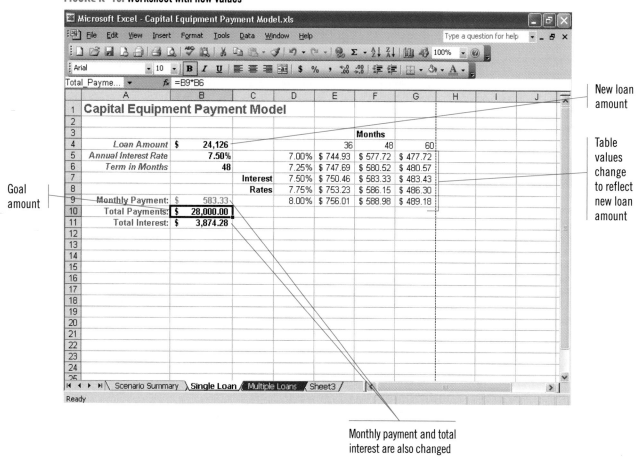

- New loan amount
- Table values change to reflect new loan amount
- Goal amount
- Monthly payment and total interest are also changed

Clues to Use

Using the Analysis ToolPak

The Analysis ToolPak is an add-in that contains many statistical analysis tools. To install the Analysis ToolPak, click Tools on the menu bar, click Add-Ins, select the Analysis ToolPak check box to select it, then click OK. To use the statistical tools, click Tools on the menu bar, click Data Analysis, click the tool that you want to use in the Data Analysis dialog box, then click OK. The Descriptive Analysis tool in the Data Analysis dialog box generates a statistical report including mean, median and mode for an input range you specify on your worksheet.

Setting up a Complex What-if Analysis with Solver

The Excel Solver finds the most appropriate value for a formula by changing the input values in the worksheet. The cell containing the formula is called the **target cell**. As you learned earlier, cells containing the values that change are called "changing cells." Solver is helpful when you need to perform a complex what-if analysis involving multiple input values or when the input values must conform to specific constraints. ▰▰▰▰ After seeing the analysis of interest rates and payments, Jim decides to review the vehicle purchase order for the MediaLoft shuttle service. He decides that the best plan is to purchase a combination of vans, sedans, and compact cars that can accommodate a total of 44 passengers. The total monthly payments for the vehicles should not exceed $3600. You use Solver to help Jim find the best possible combination of vehicles.

STEPS

TROUBLE
If Solver is not on your Tools menu, install the Solver add-in. Click Tools, click Add-Ins, then select the Solver Add-in check box.

1. **Click the** Multiple Loans sheet tab

   See Figure K-17. This worksheet is designed to calculate the total loan amount, total monthly payments, and total number of passengers for a combination of vans, sedans, and compact cars. It assumes an annual interest rate of 7% and a loan term of 48 months. You use Solver to change the purchase quantities in cells B7:D7 (the changing cells) to achieve your target of 44 passengers in cell B15 (the target cell). Your want your solution to include a constraint on cell B14, specifying that the total monthly payments must be less than or equal to $3600.

TROUBLE
If your Solver Parameters dialog box has entries in the By Changing Cells box or in the Subject to the Constraints box, click Reset All, click OK, then continue with Step 3.

2. **Click** Tools **on the menu bar, then click** Solver

   The Solver Parameters dialog box opens. This is where you indicate the target cell, the changing cells, and the constraints under which you want Solver to work. You begin by changing the value in the target cell.

3. **With the** Set Target Cell text box **selected in the Solver Parameters dialog box, click cell** B15 **in the worksheet, click the** Value of option button, **double-click the** Value of text box, **then type** 44

   You have specified a target value of 44 for the total number of passengers.

4. **Select the text in the By Changing Cells text box, then select cells** B7:D7 **in the worksheet**

   You have told Excel which cells to vary to reach the goal of 44 passengers. You need to specify the constraints on the worksheet values to restrict the Solver answer to realistic values.

5. **Click** Add, **with the insertion point in the Cell Reference text box in the Add Constraint dialog box, click cell** B14 **in the worksheet, click the list arrow in the dialog box, select** <=, **click the** Constraint text box, **type** 3600

   See Figure K-18. The Add Constraint dialog box specifies that cell B14 should contain total monthly payments that are less than or equal to 3600. Next, you need to add the constraint that the purchase quantities should be as close as possible to integers.

6. **Click** Add, **with the insertion point in the Cell Reference text box, select range** B7:D7 **in the worksheet, click the list arrow, then select** int

   Integer appears in the Constraint text box. Next, you need to specify that the purchase quantities should be greater than or equal to zero.

7. **Click** Add, **with the insertion point in the Cell Reference box, select cells** B7:D7, **select** >=, **type** 0 **in the** Constraint text box, **then click** OK

   The Solver Parameters dialog box reappears, with the constraints listed as shown in Figure K-19. In the next lesson, you run Solver and generate an Answer Report.

FIGURE K-17: Worksheet set up for a complex what-if analysis

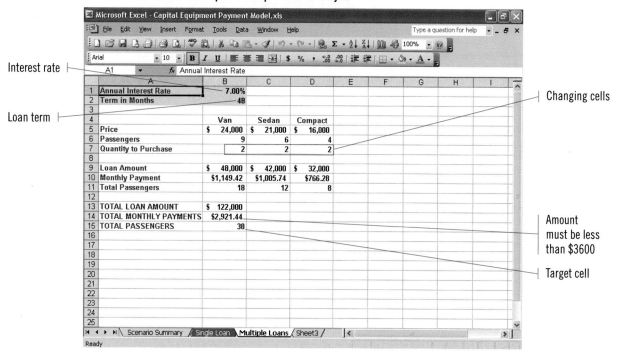

FIGURE K-18: Adding constraints

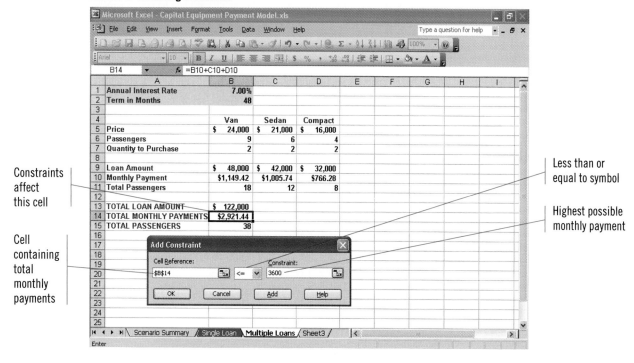

FIGURE K-19: Completed Solver Parameters dialog box

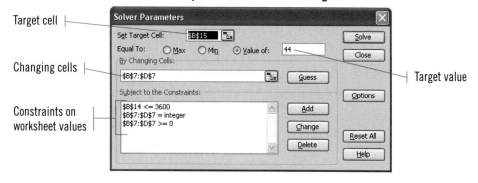

Running Solver and Generating an Answer Report

After entering all the parameters in the Solver Parameters dialog box, you can run Solver to find a solution. In some cases, Solver may not be able to find a solution that meets all of your constraints; then you would need to enter new constraints and try again. Once Solver finds a solution, you can choose to create a special report displaying the solution. You have finished entering the parameters in the Solver Parameters dialog box. Jim wants you to run Solver and create an Answer Report.

STEPS

1. **Make sure your Solver Parameters dialog box matches Figure K-19 in the previous lesson**

2. **Click** Solve

    After a moment, the Solver Results dialog box opens, indicating that Solver has found a solution. See Figure K-20. The solution values appear in the worksheet, but you decide to move them to a special Answer Report and display the original values in the worksheet.

3. **Click the** Restore Original Values option button, **click** Answer **in the Reports list box, then click** OK

    The Solver Results dialog box closes, and the original values appear in the worksheet. The Answer Report appears on a separate sheet.

4. **Click the** Answer Report 1 sheet tab

    The Answer Report displays the solution to the vehicle-purchasing problem, as shown in Figure K-21. To accommodate 44 passengers and keep the monthly payments under $3600, you need to purchase two vans, three sedans, and two compact cars. Solver's solution includes two long decimals, in cells E8 and E14, that are so small as to be insignificant. Additionally, the Original Value column in the Answer Report doesn't contain any useful information.

5. **Click cell** E8, **press [Ctrl], click cell** E14, **click the** Decrease Decimal button 📉 **on the Formatting toolbar until the cells display no decimal places, right-click the** column D heading, **then click** Delete **in the shortcut menu**

6. **Return to cell A1, enter your name in the left section of the report footer, save the workbook, then preview and print the report**

    The Answer Report displays the Final Values for the number of vehicles as integers. See Figure K-22. You've successfully found the best combination of vehicles using Solver. The settings you specified in the Solver Parameters for the Multiple Loans worksheet are saved along with the workbook.

7. **Close the workbook and exit Excel**

FIGURE K-20: Solver Results dialog box

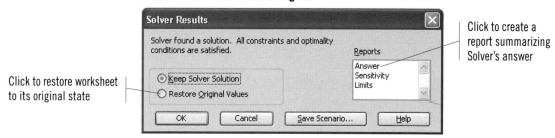

Click to restore worksheet to its original state

Click to create a report summarizing Solver's answer

FIGURE K-21: Answer Report

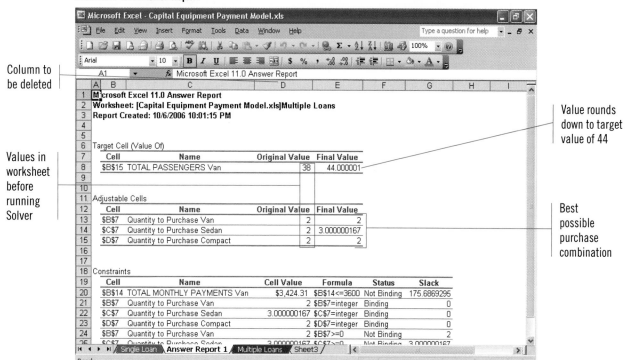

Column to be deleted

Values in worksheet before running Solver

Value rounds down to target value of 44

Best possible purchase combination

FIGURE K-22: Completed Answer Report

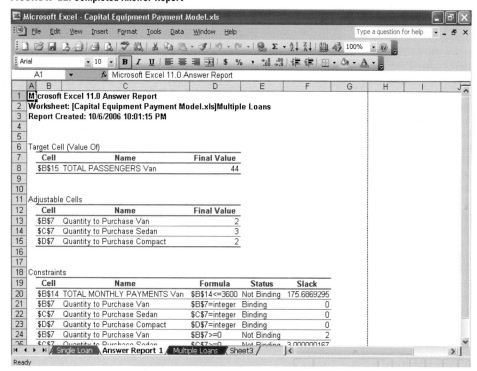

Practice

▼ CONCEPTS REVIEW

FIGURE K-23

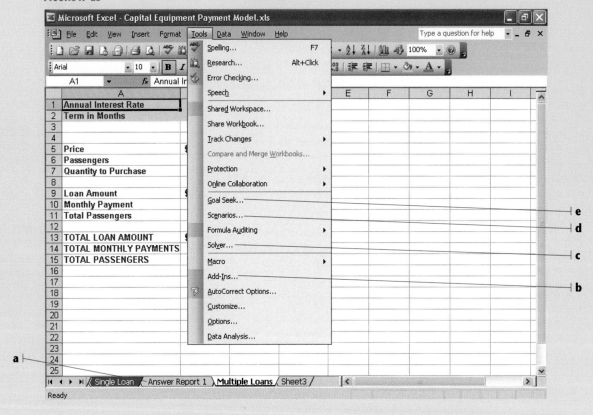

1. Which element do you click to perform a what-if analysis?
2. Which element do you click to find the input values that produce a specified result?
3. Which element is the result of running Solver?
4. Which element do you click to find a solution that meets certain constraints by changing input values in the worksheet?
5. Which element do you click to install Solver if it does not appear on the Tools menu?

Match each term with the statement that best describes it.

6. Goal Seek
7. Solver
8. Two-input data table
9. One-input data table
10. Scenario summary

a. Add-in that helps you solve complex what-if scenarios with multiple input values
b. Separate sheet with results from the worksheet's scenarios
c. Generates values resulting from varying two sets of changing values in a formula
d. Helps you backsolve what-if scenarios
e. Generates values resulting from varying one set of changing values in a formula

Select the best answer from the list of choices.

11. To hide the contents of a cell from view, you can use the custom number format:
   a. —
   b. ""
   c. ;;;
   d. Blank

12. The integer constraint can be added to cells in the Solver Parameters dialog box by choosing:
   a. int
   b. **.**
   c. **
   d. **.00

13. When you use Goal Seek, you specify a _____, then find the values that produce it.
   a. Solution
   b. Changing value
   c. Row input cell
   d. Column input cell

14. In Solver, the cell containing the formula is called the:
   a. Target cell
   b. Input cell
   c. Output cell
   d. Changing cell

▼ SKILLS REVIEW

1. **Define a what-if analysis.**
   a. Start Excel, open the Data File EX K-2.xls from the drive and folder where your Data Files are stored, then save it as **Capital Equipment Repair Model**.
   b. With the Cappuccino Machine Repair worksheet displayed, state the purpose of the worksheet model.
   c. Locate the data input cells.
   d. Locate any dependent cells.
   e. Write three questions that this what-if analysis model could answer.

2. **Track a what-if analysis with Scenario Manager.**
   a. Set up the most likely scenario with the current data input values. Select the range B3:B5, then create a scenario called **Most Likely**.
   b. Add a scenario called **Best Case** using the same changing cells, but change the Labor cost per hr. in the $B$3 text box to **70**, change the Parts cost per job in the $B$4 text box to **60**, then change the Hrs. per job value in cell $B$5 to **1**.
   c. Add a scenario called **Worst Case**. For this scenario, change the Labor cost per hr. in the $B$3 text box to **90**, change the Parts cost per job in the $B$4 text box **70**, then change the Hrs. per job in the $B$5 text box to 3.
   d. If necessary, drag the Scenario Manager dialog box to the right until columns A and B are visible.
   e. Show the Worst Case scenario results.
   f. Show the Best Case scenario results. Finally, display the Most Likely scenario results.
   g. Close the Scenario Manager dialog box.
   h. Save the workbook.

3. **Generate a scenario summary.**
   a. Create names for the input value cells and the dependent cell in the range A3:B7 (based on the left column).
   b. Verify that the names were created.
   c. Create a scenario summary report using the Cost to complete job value in cell B7 as the result cell.
   d. Edit the title of the Summary report in cell B2 to read **Scenario Summary for Cappuccino Machine Repair**.
   e. Delete the Current Values column.
   f. Delete the notes beginning in cell B11.
   g. Return to cell A1, enter your name in the left section of the Scenario Summary sheet footer, save the workbook, then preview and print the Scenario Summary sheet.

4. Project figures using a data table.

  a. Click the Cappuccino Machine Repair sheet tab.

  b. Enter the label **Labor $** in cell D3.

  c. Format the label so that it is boldfaced and right-aligned.

  d. In cell D4, enter **70**; then in cell D5, enter **75**.

  e. Select range D4:D5, then use the fill handle to extend the series to cell D8.

  f. In cell E3, reference the job cost formula by entering **=B7**.

  g. Format the contents of cell E3 as hidden, using the ;;; Custom formatting type on the Number tab of the Format Cells dialog box.

  h. Generate the new job costs based on the varying labor costs: select range D3:E8 and create a data table. In the Table dialog box, make cell B3, the labor cost, the column input cell.

  i. Format range E4:E8 as currency.

  j. Enter your name in the worksheet footer, save the workbook, then preview and print the worksheet.

5. Create a two-input data table.

  a. Move the contents of cell D3 to cell C6.

  b. Delete the contents of range E4:E8, but do not clear the formatting.

  c. Format cell E3 using the General category on the Number tab of the Format Cells dialog box, then move the contents of cell E3 to cell D3.

  d. Format the contents of cell D3 as hidden, using the ;;; Custom formatting type on the Number tab of the Format Cells dialog box.

  e. Enter **Hours per job** in cell F2, and format it so it is boldfaced.

  f. Enter **1** in cell E3, enter **1.5** in cell F3, then enter **2** in cell G3.

  g. Select range D3:G8 and create a data table, making cell B5 the row input cell and cell B3 the column input cell.

  h. Format the range F4:G8 as currency.

  i. Save the workbook, then preview and print the worksheet.

6. Use Goal Seek.

  a. Click cell B7, and open the Goal Seek dialog box.

  b. Determine what the parts would have to cost so that the cost to complete the job is $160. Enter a job cost of **160** as the To value, and enter **B4** (the Parts cost) as the By changing cell; write down the parts cost that Goal Seek finds.

  c. Click OK, then use **[Ctrl][Z]** to reset the parts cost to its original value.

  d. Enter the cost of the parts in cell B14.

  e. Determine what the labor would have to cost so that the cost to complete the job is $155. Use **[Ctrl][Z]** to reset the labor cost to its original value. Enter the labor cost in cell B15.

  f. Save the workbook, then preview and print the worksheet.

7. Perform a complex what-if analysis with Solver and generate an Answer Report.

  a. Click the Vehicle Repair sheet tab to make it active, then open the Solver dialog box.

  b. Make B14 (the total repair costs) the target cell, with a target value of 13000.

  c. Use cells B6:D6, the number of scheduled repairs, as the changing cells.

  d. Specify that cells B6:D6 must be integers and greater than or equal to zero.

  e. Use Solver to find a solution.

  f. Generate an Answer Report and restore the original values to the worksheet.

  g. Edit the Answer Report to delete the original values column.

  h. Enter your name in the left section of the report footer, save the workbook, then preview and print the Answer Report.

  i. Close the workbook then exit Excel.

▼ INDEPENDENT CHALLENGE 1

You are a sales representative for Ed-Toys, a toy company located in Minneapolis, Minnesota. Your sales territory includes five states in the Midwest. You submit a monthly expense report detailing car expenses calculated on a mileage basis. Your vehicle expenses have been increasing as your sales territory has grown. Your sales manager has asked you to research the monthly cost of purchasing a company car to see if it is more economical than expensing vehicle costs on your own car. You have created a preliminary worksheet model to determine the monthly payments for a $20,000 car, based on several different interest rates and loan terms using data from the company's bank. You will compare two-, three-, and four-year car loans. Using Scenario Manager, you create the following three scenarios: a four-year loan at 5.0%; a three-year loan at 4.75%; and a two-year loan at 4.5%. You prepare a scenario summary report for your manager showing the payment details.

a. Start Excel, open the Data File EX K-3.xls from the drive and folder where your Data Files are stored, then save it as **Car Loan Payment Model**.

b. Create cell names for the cells B4:B11 based on the labels in cells A4:A11, using the Name option on the Insert menu.

c. You use Scenario Manager to calculate the monthly payment on a $20,000 loan under three sets of loan possibilities. Create the following three scenarios, using cells B5:B6 as the changing cells for each one. Enter the interest rate in the first Scenario values text box and the number of months in the second Scenario values text box.

Scenario Name	Interest Rate	Term
5.0 percent	.05	48
4.75 percent	.0475	36
4.5 percent	.045	24

d. Show each scenario to make sure it performs as intended, then display the 5.0 percent scenario.

e. Generate a scenario summary titled **Scenario Summary for $20,000 Car Purchase**. Use cells B9:B11 as the Result cells.

f. Delete the Current Values column in the report. Delete the notes at the bottom of the report.

g. Enter your name in the left section of the Scenario Summary sheet footer. Save the workbook, preview, then print the scenario summary.

Advanced Challenge Exercise

- Create a copy of the Loan sheet using the Move or Copy Sheet option on the Edit menu. Delete the existing scenarios in the copied sheet.

- Create a new scenario in the copied sheet called **My Loan** using an interest rate and term available at a local lending institution.

- Merge the scenarios from the Loan sheet into the new sheet. (*Hint*: Use the Merge option in the Scenario Manager dialog box.)

- Generate a scenario summary titled **Advanced Scenario Summary** using cells B9:B11 as the Result cells. Delete the Current Values column in the report and the notes at the bottom.

- Enter your name in the left section of the Scenario Summary2 sheet footer, save the workbook, preview then print the Advanced Scenario Summary in landscape orientation.

h. Close the workbook, then exit Excel.

▼ INDEPENDENT CHALLENGE 2

You are a senior staff associate at Capital Adventures, a venture capital firm located in Albany, New York. One of the vice presidents has asked you to prepare a loan summary report for a software development company seeking capital for a business expansion. You need to develop a model to show what the monthly payments would be for a $900,000 loan, over 5- and 10-year terms, with interest rates ranging in 0.25% increments. You first create a two-input data table that shows the results of varying loan term and interest rates, then you use Goal Seek to specify a total payment amount for this loan application.

a. Start Excel, open the Data File EX K-4.xls from the drive and folder where your Data Files are stored, then save it as **Capital Loan Payment Model**.

b. Reference the monthly payment amount from cell B9 in cell D4, and format the contents of cell D4 as hidden.

▼ INDEPENDENT CHALLENGE 2 (CONTINUED)

c. Using cells D4:F13, create a two-input data table structure with varying interest rates for 5- and 10-year terms. Use cells D5:D13 for the interest rates, with 5% as the lowest possible rate and 7% the highest. Vary the rates in between by 0.25%. Use Figure K-24 as a guide.

d. Generate the data table that shows the effect of varying interest rates and loan terms on the monthly payments. Use cell B6, Term in Months, as the row input cell, and cell B5, the Annual Interest Rate, as the column input cell. Format cells E5:F13 as currency.

FIGURE K-24

	A	B	C	D	E	F	G
1	Capital Adventures						
2							
3					Terms		
4	Loan Amount	$ 900,000			60	120	
5	Annual Interest Rate	6.00%		5.00%			
6	Term in Months	60		5.25%			
7				5.50%			
8				5.75%			
9	Monthly Payment:	$ 17,399.52		6.00%			
10	Total Payments:	$1,043,971.28		6.25%			
11	Total Interest:	$ 143,971.28		6.50%			
12				6.75%			
13				7.00%			

e. Select cell **B10** and use Goal Seek to find the interest rate necessary for a total payment amount of $1,000,000. Use cell B5, the Annual Interest Rate, as the By changing cell. Accept the solution found by Goal Seek.

f. Enter your name in the worksheet footer, save the workbook, then preview and print the worksheet.

g. Close the workbook, then exit Excel.

▼ INDEPENDENT CHALLENGE 3

You are the owner of Computer City, a small computer store, where you custom configure PCs to sell to the home and business markets. You have created a financial model to determine the costs and profits associated with your three most popular configurations: PC-1, PC-2, and PC-3. You want to show how the hourly labor cost affects the total profit for each PC model your company produces. To do this, you use Goal Seek. You also want to do a what-if analysis regarding the effect of hours per unit on total profit. You decide to solve the problem by using Solver, where you can specify multiple constraints for the solution. Finally, you produce an Answer Report summarizing your analysis.

a. Start Excel, open the Data File EX K-5.xls from the drive and folder where your Data Files are stored, then save it as **PC Production Model**.

b. Enter the labels shown in cells A12:A14 in Figure K-25.

c. Use Goal Seek to find the hourly labor cost that produces a total profit for model PC-1 of $15,000. In cell D12, record the labor cost next to the label in cell A12, then reset the labor cost to its original value.

FIGURE K-25

	A	B	C	D	E	F	G	H	I
1	Computer City								
2	Hourly labor cost	80							
3	Component cost	75							
4									
5		Hours per Unit	Components per Unit	Cost to Produce	Retail Price	Unit Profit	Units Produced	Total Profit	
6	PC-1	4.00	6	770	995	225	53	11,925	
7	PC-2	3.00	9	915	1,200	285	75	21,375	
8	PC-3	5.00	12	1,300	1,600	300	62	18,600	
9								51,900	
10									
11									
12	Labor cost for $15,000 profit for PC-1								
13	Labor cost for $25,000 profit for PC-2								
14	Labor cost for $20,000 profit for PC-3								
15									

d. Use Goal Seek to find the hourly labor cost that produces a total profit for model PC-2 of $25,000. In cell D13, record the labor cost next to the label in cell A13, then reset the labor cost to its original value.

e. Use Goal Seek to find the hourly labor cost that produces a total profit for model PC-3 of $20,000. In cell D14, record the labor cost next to the label in cell A14, then reset the labor cost to its original value.

f. Format your labor costs in cells D12:D14 as currency.

g. Use Solver to set the total profit of all configurations to $75,000. Use the hours per unit, cells B6:B8, as the changing cells. Specify that cells B6:B8 must be greater than or equal to 0 and less than or equal to 5.

▼ INDEPENDENT CHALLENGE 3 (CONTINUED)

h. Generate an Answer Report and restore the original values in the worksheet.

Advanced Challenge Exercise

■ To complete this Advanced Challenge Exercise, you will need to use the Descriptive Analysis tool. If the Descriptive Analysis command does not appear on your Tools menu, install the Analysis ToolPak add-in: Click Tools on the menu bar, click Add-Ins, click to place a check mark next to Analysis ToolPak, then click OK.

■ Return to the Model worksheet and use the Descriptive Statistics tool in the Data Analysis dialog box to produce a summary statistical analysis of the total profits for the three PC models. (*Hint*: Use the Data Analysis command on the Tools menu and select Descriptive Statistics. Use Figure K-26 as a guide to enter the Input Range. Notice that Grouped by Columns, Labels in First Row, New Worksheet, and Summary statistics are selected.)

FIGURE K-26

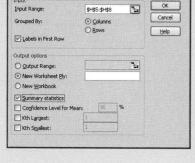

■ Adjust the column widths as necessary to display the statistical information. Use yellow as a fill color to emphasize the cells that contain mean and median profit information. Format the mean and median profit cells as currency with zero decimal places.

i. Enter your name in the left footer section of each worksheet. Save the workbook, then preview and print each sheet each on one page.

j. Close the workbook then exit Excel.

▼ INDEPENDENT CHALLENGE 4

You are the vice president of marketing for E-Learn, a distance learning consulting firm. You will be relocating to Toronto, Ontario, to set up the first Canadian office. You have sold your house and plan to use the $100,000 in equity to purchase a $200,000 home in Toronto. You will research mortgage rates for Toronto banks and mortgage brokers on the Web finding 7-year and 10-year interest rates. You'll enter the rates in a worksheet and use them to estimate monthly housing payments. You have created a preliminary worksheet model to determine these monthly payments and will investigate the effect of rate changes on your monthly payments.

a. Use the search engine of your choice to find 7-year and 10-year mortgage rates at a Toronto bank or mortgage broker.

b. Start Excel, open the Data File EX K-6.xls from the drive and folder where your Data Files are stored, then save it as **Mortgage Research**.

c. Use the Rates worksheet to enter one of the rates you found for a 7-year mortgage.

d. Create a data table structure for the worksheet with varying interest rates for 7-year and 10-year terms. Begin with a rate at least 1% lower than the 7-year rate you found as the lowest possible rate. Make the highest possible interest rate at least 1% greater than the 10-year rate you found, and vary the rates in between by 0.25%. Use Figure K-27 as a guide, using the rates you found. Use bold formatting as shown in the figure.

FIGURE K-27

	A	B	C	D	E	F	G
1	Mortgage Loan Payment Model						
2							
3	Home Price	$ 200,000			Term		
4	Down Payment	$ 100,000			84	120	
5	Loan Amount	$ 100,000		5.85%			
6	Annual Interest Rate	6.85%		6.10%			
7	Term in Months	84		6.35%			
8				6.60%			
9				6.85%			
10	Monthly Payment:	$ 1,501.95		7.10%			
11	Total Payments:	$ 126,163.46		7.35%			
12	Total Interest:	$ 26,163.46		7.60%			
13				7.85%			
14				8.10%			
15				8.35%			
16				8.60%			

e. Reference the monthly payment cell in the table and format it as hidden.

f. Generate a two-input data table for the worksheet. Use cell B7 as the row input cell and B6 as the column input cell.

g. You decide that you want to limit your housing payments to $1000 per month. You can accomplish this by using some of your savings to increase your down payment. Find the down payment amount that reduces your monthly payments to $1000 using the data and formulas in B3:B10 and Goal Seek. Make a note of the down payment amount then restore the worksheet to its original values. Record the answer found by Goal Seek in cell A20 of the worksheet.

h. Enter your name in the left section of the worksheet footer, save the workbook, then preview and print the worksheet.

i. Close the workbook, then exit Excel.

▼ VISUAL WORKSHOP

Create the worksheet shown in Figure K-28. Make sure to generate all three tables as data tables. Save the workbook as **Notebook Payment Model**. Add your name to the footer, then preview and print the worksheet in landscape orientation. Print the worksheet again with the formulas displayed.

FIGURE K-28

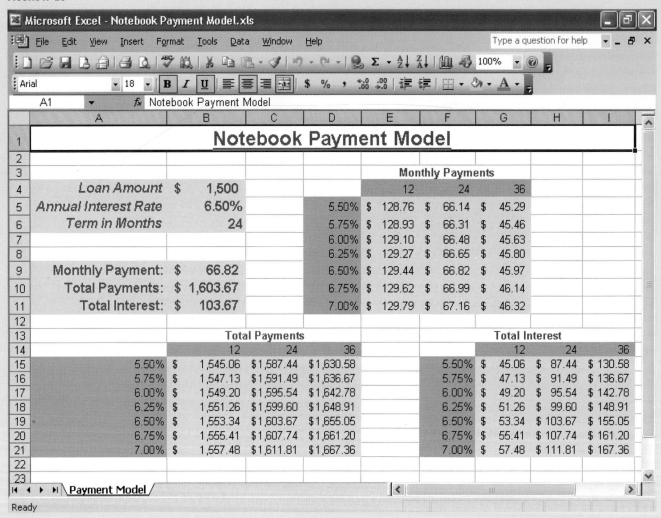

UNIT
L
Excel 2003

Analyzing Data with PivotTables

OBJECTIVES

Plan and design a PivotTable report

Create a PivotTable report

Change the summary function of a PivotTable report

Analyze three-dimensional data

Update a PivotTable report

Change the structure and format of a PivotTable report

Create a PivotChart report

Use the GETPIVOTDATA function

If you have a SAM user profile, you may have access to hands-on instruction, practice, and assessment of the skills covered in this unit. Log in to your SAM account and go to your assignments page to see what your instructor has assigned.

The Excel **PivotTable** feature lets you summarize selected worksheet data in an interactive table format. You can freely rearrange, or "pivot," parts of the table structure around the data and summarize any data values within the table by category. You also can view data three-dimensionally, with data for each category arranged in a stack of pages. There are two PivotTable features in Excel: PivotTable reports and PivotChart reports. In this unit, you will plan, design, create, update, and change the layout and format of a PivotTable report. You will also add a page field to a PivotTable report, then create a PivotChart report. ▓▓▓ The Sales Department is getting ready for its annual meeting and the eastern regional sales manager has asked Jim Fernandez, the marketing director for MediaLoft, to develop an analysis of products sold in its Boston, New York, and Washington, DC, stores over the past year. Jim asks you to create a PivotTable to summarize the 2006 sales data by quarter, product, and city.

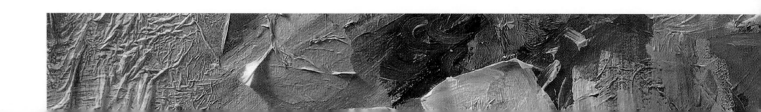

Planning and Designing a PivotTable Report

Creating a **PivotTable report** (often called a PivotTable) involves only a few steps. Before you begin, however, you need to review the data and consider how a PivotTable can best summarize it.  Jim asks you to design a PivotTable to display MediaLoft's sales information for its eastern cities. You begin by reviewing guidelines for creating PivotTables.

DETAILS

Before you create a PivotTable, think about the following guidelines:

- **Review the source data**

  Before you can effectively summarize data in a PivotTable, you need to understand the source data's scope and structure. The source data does not have to be defined as a list, but should be in a list-like format. That is, it should not have any blank rows or columns, and should have the same type of data in each column. There should be repeated information in one or more fields in order for the PivotTable to effectively group it. There should also be numeric data that the PivotTable can total for each group. The data columns represent categories of data, which are called fields, just as in a list. You are working with product sales information that Jim received from MediaLoft's eastern region sales manager. This list is shown in Figure L-1. Notice that there is repeated information in the Item, City, and Quarter columns, so you will be able to summarize this data effectively in a PivotTable.

- **Determine the purpose of the PivotTable and write down the names of the fields you want to include**

  The purpose of your PivotTable is to summarize sales information by quarter across various cities. You will include the following fields in the PivotTable: Product ID, Item, City, Quarter, and Sales.

- **Determine which field contains the data you want to summarize and which summary function you want to use**

  You want to summarize sales information by summing the sales field for each product in a city by quarter. You'll do this by using the Excel SUM function.

- **Decide how you want to arrange the data**

  The layout of a PivotTable is crucial in delivering its intended message. Product ID will appear in the PivotTable columns, City, and Quarter will appear in rows, and the PivotTable will summarize Sales figures. See Figure L-2.

- **Determine the location of the PivotTable**

  You can place a PivotTable in any worksheet of any workbook. Placing a PivotTable on a separate worksheet makes it easier to locate, however, and prevents you from accidentally overwriting parts of an existing sheet. You decide to create the PivotTable as a new worksheet in the current workbook.

FIGURE L-1: Sales worksheet

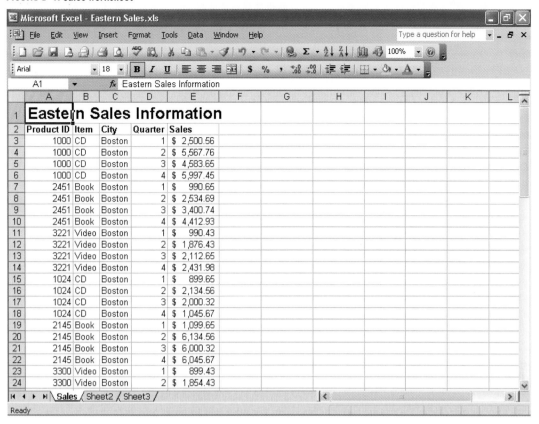

FIGURE L-2: Example of a PivotTable report

Product ID values appear in column area

Cities appear in row area

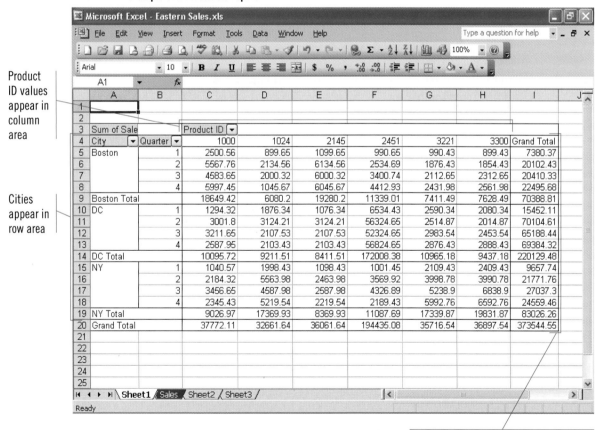

Sales figures are summarized in the data area

Creating a PivotTable Report

Once you've planned and designed your PivotTable, you can create it. The PivotTable Wizard takes you through the process step by step. With the planning and design stage complete, you are ready to create a PivotTable that summarizes sales information. The sales managers in Boston, New York, and Washington, DC will use this information to develop a marketing plan for the coming year.

STEPS

1. **Start Excel if necessary, open the Data File EX L-1.xls from the drive and folder where your Data Files are stored, then save it as Eastern Sales**

   This worksheet contains the year's sales information for MediaLoft's eastern region, including Product ID, Item, City, Quarter, and Sales. Notice that the records are sorted by city.

2. **Select cell A1 if necessary, click Data on the menu bar, then click PivotTable and PivotChart Report**

   The first PivotTable and PivotChart Wizard dialog box opens, as shown in Figure L-3. This is where you specify the type of data source you want to use for your PivotTable: an Excel list or database, an external data source (for example, a Microsoft Access file), or multiple consolidation ranges (worksheet ranges). You also have the option of creating a PivotTable or PivotChart report.

3. **Make sure the Microsoft Office Excel list or database option button is selected, make sure PivotTable is selected, then click Next**

   The second PivotTable and PivotChart Wizard dialog box opens. Because the cell pointer was located within the list before you opened the PivotTable Wizard, Excel automatically completes the Range box with the table range that includes the selected cell—in this case, $A$2:$E$74.

4. **Click Next**

   The third PivotTable and PivotChart Wizard dialog box opens. You use this dialog box to specify where you want to place the PivotTable.

TROUBLE

To display the PivotTable toolbar, click View on the menu bar, point to Toolbars, then click PivotTable to select it.

5. **Make sure New Worksheet is selected, click Finish, then drag your Field List window and PivotTable toolbar to the locations shown in Figure L-4**

   The **PivotTable toolbar** contains buttons that allow you to manipulate data. The PivotTable Field List window contains field names that you can add to the PivotTable by adding them into various "drop areas" of the PivotTable or by using the Add To button at the bottom of the list window.

6. **Click the Product ID field in the PivotTable Field List, click the list arrow at the bottom of the window, choose Column Area, then click the Add To button; click the City field in the PivotTable Field List, click the list arrow at the bottom of the window, choose Row Area, then click the Add To button; click the Quarter field in the PivotTable Field List, verify that Row Area is selected, then click the Add To button**

   The Quarter field is added to the right of the City field in the Row Area. You have created a PivotTable with the Product IDs as column headers and Cities and Quarters as row labels.

QUICK TIP

To remove a field from a PivotTable, drag it outside of the PivotTable area.

7. **Click the Sales field in the PivotTable Field List, click the list arrow at the bottom of the window, choose Data Area, then click the Add To button**

   Because SUM is the Excel default function for data fields containing numbers, Excel automatically calculates the sum of the sales by product ID and by city and quarter. The PivotTable tells you that Product #1000 Boston sales were twice the New York sales level. Product 2451 was the best selling product overall, as you can see in the grand total row. See Figure L-5.

8. **Save the workbook**

FIGURE L-3: First PivotTable Wizard dialog box

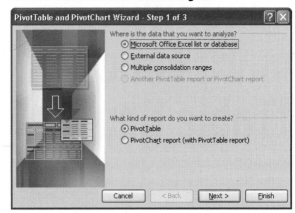

FIGURE L-4: New PivotTable ready to receive field data

PivotTable Field List window

"Drop" indicates that you can drag and drop fields to these areas instead of using the Field List

Your field list may be a different size

PivotTable toolbar

Click to select PivotTable area in which to place selected field

Click to add selected field to PivotTable

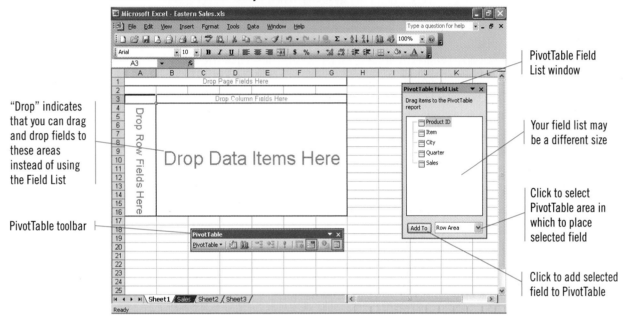

FIGURE L-5: New PivotTable with fields in place

Boston sales for this product were twice as high as New York sales

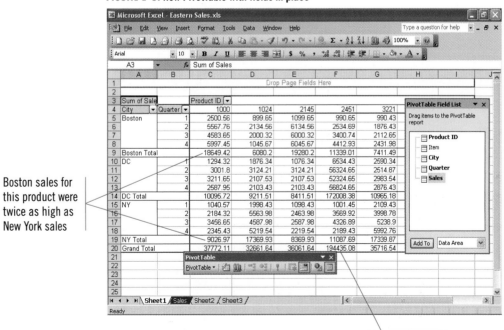

Product 2451 outsold all products

Changing the Summary Function of a PivotTable Report

A PivotTable's **summary function** controls how Excel calculates the table data. Unless you specify otherwise, Excel applies the SUM function to numeric data and the COUNT function to data fields containing text. However, you can easily change the SUM function to a different summary function, such as AVERAGE, which calculates the average of all values in the field. ▰▰▰▰▰ Jim wants you to calculate the average sales for the northeastern cities using the AVERAGE function.

STEPS

1. **Click any cell in the data area (A3:I20), then click the Field Settings button 🔲 on the PivotTable toolbar**

   The PivotTable toolbar buttons are described in Table L-1. The PivotTable Field dialog box opens. The selected function in the Summarize by list box determines how the data is calculated.

2. **In the Summarize by list box, click Average, then click OK**

   The PivotTable Field dialog box closes. The data area of the PivotTable shows the average sales for each product by city and quarter. See Figure L-6. After reviewing the data, you decide that it would be more useful to sum the salary information than to average it.

   QUICK TIP

   When you name a PivotTable sheet, it is best to avoid using spaces in the name. If a PivotTable name contains a space, you must put single quotes around the name when you refer to it in a function.

3. **Click 🔲 on the PivotTable toolbar; in the Summarize by list box, click Sum, then click OK**

   The PivotTable Field dialog box closes and Excel recalculates the PivotTable—this time, summing the sales data instead of averaging it.

4. **Rename Sheet1 PivotTable, add your name to the worksheet footer, then save the workbook and print the worksheet in landscape orientation.**

TABLE L-1: PivotTable toolbar buttons

button	name	description
PivotTable ▾	PivotTable Menu	Displays menu of PivotTable commands
🔲	Format Report	Displays a list of PivotTable AutoFormats
🔲	Chart Wizard	Creates a PivotChart report
🔲	Hide Detail	Hides detail in table groupings
🔲	Show Detail	Shows detail in table groupings
🔲	Refresh Data	Updates list changes within the table
🔲	Include Hidden Items in Totals	Includes values for all items in totals, including hidden items
🔲	Always Display Items	Turns on drop-down selections for PivotTable fields
🔲	Field Settings	Displays a list of field settings
🔲	Show/Hide Field List	Displays/hides PivotTable Field List window; in a chart, displays or hides outlines and labels

FIGURE L-6: PivotTable showing averages

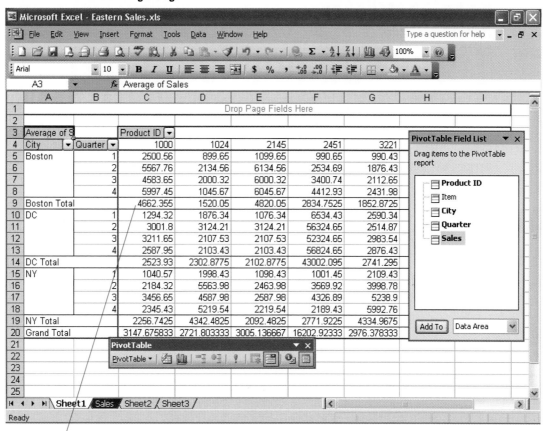

Boston Average for
Product ID 1000

Clues to Use

Changing PivotTable report field names

You can make your PivotTable report easier to read by changing the field names to more descriptive names. You can rename a field by double-clicking the field name to open the PivotTable Field List dialog box and entering the new field name in the Name textbox. This only changes the name in the PivotTable, not in the Field List. You can also rename a field by clicking the field name and then clicking the Field Settings button on the PivotTable toolbar to open the PivotTable Field dialog box.

Analyzing Three-dimensional Data

When you place row and column fields to create a PivotTable, you are working with two-dimensional data. You can convert a PivotTable to a three-dimensional data analysis tool by adding a page field. A **page field** makes the data appear as if it is stacked in pages, thus adding a third dimension to the analysis. When using a page field, you are in effect filtering data through that field.  Jim wants you to filter the PivotTable so that only one quarter's data is visible at one time.

STEPS

> **TROUBLE**
> If the Quarter field was not added to the PivotTable, redo Step 1, making sure you click the Quarter field in the Field List.

1. **Click the** Quarter field name **in the PivotTable Field List, click the list arrow in the lower-right corner of the field list, select** Page Area**, click** Add To

   The PivotTable is re-created with a page field showing data for all the quarters. You can easily view the data for each quarter.

> **QUICK TIP**
> To display each page of the page field on a separate worksheet, click PivotTable on the PivotTable toolbar, click Show Pages, then click OK.

2. **In the PivotTable cell B1, click the** Quarter list arrow

   Each quarter is listed in addition to an option to show All quarters. See Figure L-7.

3. **Click** 1**, then click** OK

   The PivotTable summarizes the sales data for the first quarter only, as shown in Figure L-8.

4. **Click the** Quarter list arrow**, click** 4**, then click** OK

   The sales for the fourth quarter appear.

5. **Save the workbook**

Clues to Use

Customizing PivotTables

You can customize the default Excel PivotTable to show information in a format that is appropriate for your particular audience. To modify the order of items in the table, right-click a cell, then use the commands on the Order submenu to reorder the selected item(s).

To add or hide detail, right-click a cell, then use the commands on the Group and Show Detail submenu to expand, display, or hide more detail. When you show details of a selected area, Excel creates a new worksheet containing the detail you requested.

FIGURE L-7: PivotTable with Quarter as a page field

Click a quarter to view its data

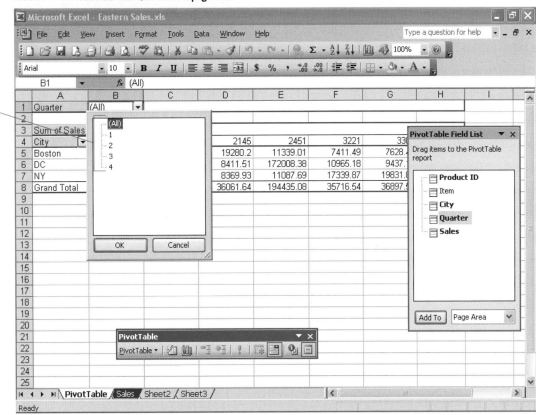

FIGURE L-8: PivotTable filtered to show only first quarter sales

Quarter field specifies that only the first quarter should be displayed

Sales for first quarter only

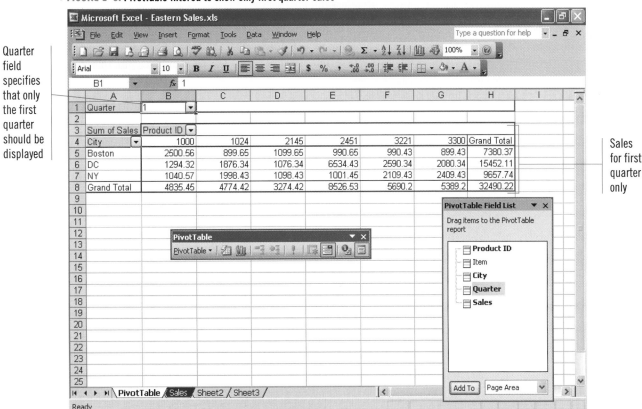

Excel 2003

Updating a PivotTable Report

The data in a PivotTable report looks like typical worksheet data. Because the PivotTable data is linked to a **source list** (the list data you used to create the PivotTable), however, the values and results in the PivotTable are read-only values. That means you cannot move or modify a part of a PivotTable by inserting or deleting rows, editing results, or moving cells. To change PivotTable data, you must edit the items directly in the source list, and then update, or **refresh**, the PivotTable to reflect the changes. Jim just learned that sales information for a custom CD sold in Boston during the fourth quarter was never entered into the Sales worksheet. Jim asks you to add information about this CD to the current list. You start by inserting a row for the new information in the Sales worksheet.

STEPS

1. **Click the Sales sheet tab**

   By inserting the new row in the correct position by city, you will not need to sort the list again. Also, by adding the new information within the list range, the new row data is included automatically in the list range.

2. **Right-click the row 27 heading; then on the shortcut menu, click Insert**

   A blank row appears as the new row 27, and the data in the old row 27 moves down to row 28. You enter the CD data in the new row 27.

3. **Enter the data for the new CD using the following information**

Product ID	1924
Item	CD
City	Boston
Quarter	4
Sales	2600.68

   The PivotTable does not yet reflect the additional data.

4. **Click the PivotTable sheet tab, then make sure the Quarter 4 page is displayed**

   Notice that the fourth quarter list does not currently include this new CD information and that the grand total is $116439.46. Before you refresh the PivotTable data, you need to make sure that the cell pointer is located within the PivotTable range.

   QUICK TIP

   If you want Excel to refresh your PivotTable report automatically when you open the workbook in which it is contained, click the PivotTable list arrow on the PivotTable toolbar, click Table Options, under Data source options select Refresh on open, then click OK.

5. **Click anywhere within the PivotTable, then click the Refresh Data button 🔡 on the PivotTable toolbar**

   The PivotTable now includes the new CD information in column H, and the grand total has increased by the amount of the CD's sales (2600.68) to 119040.14. See Figure L-9.

6. **Save the workbook**

FIGURE L-9: Updated PivotTable report

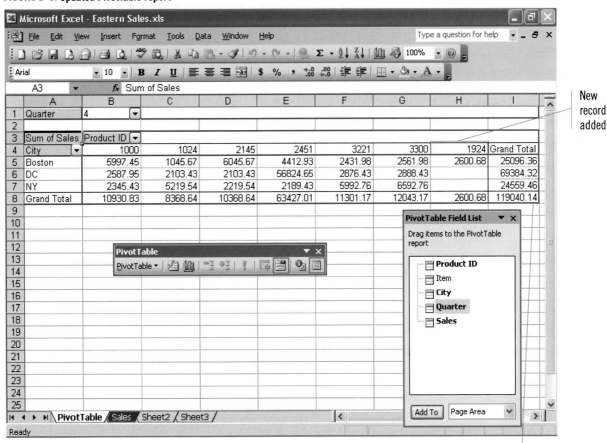

New record added

Total reflects new CD information

Clues to Use

Maintaining original table data

Once you select the Refresh Data command, you cannot undo the operation. If you want the PivotTable to display the original source data, you must change the source data list, then reselect the Refresh

Data command. If you're concerned about the effect refreshing the PivotTable might have on your work, save a second (working) copy of the workbook so that your original data remains intact.

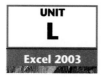
Changing the Structure and Format of a PivotTable Report

Although you cannot change the actual data in a PivotTable, you can alter its structure and appearance at any time. You might, for example, add a column field, or switch the positions of existing fields. You can quickly change the way data is displayed in a PivotTable by dragging field buttons in the worksheet from a row position to a column position, or vice versa. Alternately, you may want to enhance the appearance of a PivotTable by changing the way the text or values are formatted. It's a good idea to format a PivotTable using AutoFormat, because once you refresh a PivotTable, any formatting that has not been applied to the cells through AutoFormat is removed. ▰▰▰▰ The eastern sales manager has asked Jim to include item information in the sales report. Jim asks you to add Item as a page field and then format the PivotTable.

STEPS

1. **Make sure that the** PivotTable sheet **is active, that the active cell is located anywhere inside the PivotTable, and that the PivotTable Field List is visible**

2. **Click the** Item field **in the PivotTable Field List, verify that** Page Area **is selected, then click** Add To

   You can move fields in a PivotTable by dragging and then dropping them at the desired location. When you drag a field, the pointer appears with a PivotTable outline attached to its lower-right corner.

3. **Drag the Item field up and drop it above the Quarter field**

   The PivotTable on the pointer displays a blue box in the Page area. When you drop the field, the Item field is placed in the Page area above the Quarter Page field. See Figure L-10. Jim asks you to display the book sales information for all quarters.

4. **Click the** Item list arrow, **click** Book, **click** OK, **click the** Quarter list arrow, **click** All, **then click** OK

   You are ready to format the PivotTable.

QUICK TIP

Report formats 1–10 are indented formats, like a banded database report. Tables 1–10 are not indented. Indented reports contain only row fields, not column fields.

5. **Click any cell inside the PivotTable, click the** Field Settings button ⬚ **on the PivotTable toolbar, then click** Number **in the PivotTable Field dialog box**

6. **Under Category in the Format Cells dialog box, click** Accounting, **keep the Decimal places as** 2, **click** OK, **then click** OK **again**

   You have formatted the sales amounts with commas and dollar signs.

7. **Click the** Format Report button ⬚ **on the PivotTable toolbar bar; in the AutoFormat dialog box, scroll down and click the** Table 2 **format, click** OK, **then click outside the range to deselect it**

   You need to provide the eastern sales manager with sales information for all items.

8. **Click the** Item list arrow, **click** All, **then click** OK

   The completed PivotTable with the AutoFormat applied appears as shown in Figure L-11.

9. **Save the workbook, preview the PivotTable, then print it in landscape orientation**

FIGURE L-10: Revised PivotTable structure

Item field is
now in the
Page area

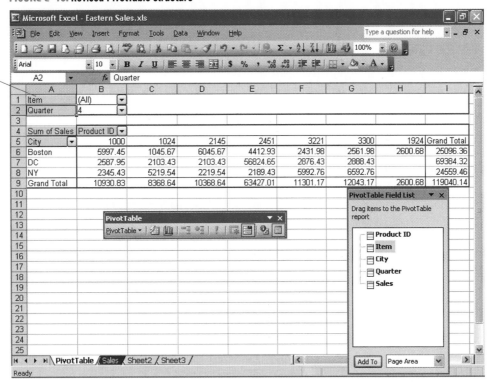

FIGURE L-11: Completed PivotTable report

AutoFormat
has applied
shading
and blue
headings

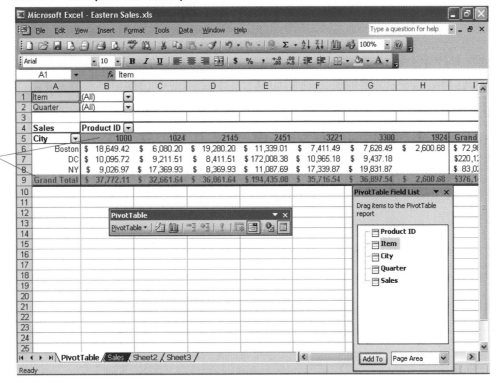

Creating a PivotChart Report

A **PivotChart report** is a chart that you create from data or from a PivotTable report. Like a PivotTable report, a PivotChart report has fields that you can move to explore new data relationships. Table L-2 describes how the elements in a PivotTable report correspond to the elements in a PivotChart report. When you create a PivotChart directly from data, Excel automatically creates a corresponding PivotTable report. When you change a PivotChart report by moving fields, Excel updates the corresponding PivotTable report to show the new layout. You can create a PivotChart report from any PivotTable report to reflect that view of your data, but if you use an indented PivotTable report format, your chart will not have series fields; indented PivotTable report formats do not include column fields. ▰▰▰▰ Jim wants you to chart the fourth quarter CD sales and the yearly CD sales average for the eastern sales manager. You use the Chart Wizard to create a Pivot Chart report from the PivotTable data.

STEPS

QUICK TIP

If your PivotTable report is an indented format, move at least one field to the column area before you create a PivotChart report to display a series field on the chart.

1. **Click the** Item list arrow, **click** CD, **click** OK, **click the** Quarter list arrow, **click** 4, **then click** OK

   The fourth quarter CD sales information appears in the PivotTable. See Figure L-12. You want to create the PivotChart from the PivotTable information you have displayed.

2. **Click any cell in the PivotTable, then click the** Chart Wizard button 🏛 **on the PivotTable toolbar**

   A new chart sheet opens with the fourth quarter CD sales displayed as a bar chart, as shown in Figure L-13. The Chart toolbar also appears. Jim wants you to change the chart to show the average sales for all quarters.

3. **Click the** Quarter list arrow **on the chart sheet, click** All, **then click** OK

   The chart now represents the sum of CD sales for the year. As with a PivotTable, you can change a PivotChart's summary function to display averages instead of totals.

QUICK TIP

You can also double-click the Sum of Sales cell to change the PivotTable's summary function.

4. **Click** Sum of Sales **above the PivotChart, click the** Field Settings button 🔲 **on the PivotTable toolbar, click** Average **in the Summarize by list, then click** OK

   The PivotChart report recalculates to display averages. The chart would be easier to understand if it had a title.

5. **Click** Chart **on the menu bar, click** Chart Options, **click the** Titles **tab if necessary, enter** Average CD Sales **in the Chart title text box, then click** OK

6. **Rename the chart sheet** PivotChart, **place your name in the chart sheet footer, save the workbook, then preview and print the PivotChart report**

   The final PivotChart report displaying the average CD sales for the year is shown in Figure L-14.

TABLE L-2: PivotTable and PivotChart elements

PivotTable items	PivotChart items
row fields	category fields
column fields	series fields
page fields	page fields

FIGURE L-12: PivotTable displaying fourth quarter CD sales

4th quarter CD sales selected

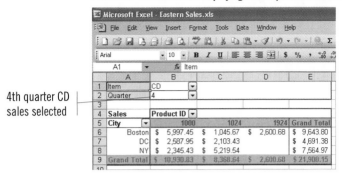

FIGURE L-13: New chart sheet displaying fourth quarter CD sales

Chart toolbar

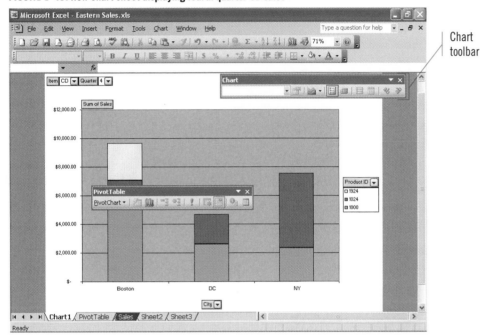

FIGURE L-14: Completed PivotChart report

Chart now shows average sales for the year

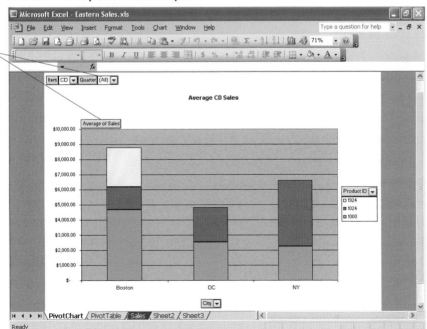

Using the GETPIVOTDATA Function

Because you can rearrange a PivotTable so easily, you can't use an ordinary cell reference when you want to reference a PivotTable cell in another worksheet. If you change the way data is displayed in a PivotTable, the data moves, rendering an ordinary cell reference incorrect. Instead, to retrieve summary data from a PivotTable, you need to use the Excel GETPIVOTDATA function. See Figure L-15 for the GETPIVOTDATA function syntax. In preparing for the Boston sales meeting, the eastern sales manager asks Jim to include the yearly sales total for the Boston store in the Sales sheet. Jim asks you to retrieve this information from the PivotTable and place it in the Sales sheet. You use the GETPIVOTDATA function to retrieve this information.

STEPS

1. **Click the PivotTable sheet tab**

   The sales figures in the PivotTable are average values for CDs. You decide to show sales information for all items and change the summary information back to Sum.

2. **Click the Item list arrow, click All, then click OK**

   The PivotChart report displays sales information for all items.

3. **Click Average of Sales on the PivotTable, click the Field Settings button on the PivotTable toolbar, click Sum in the Summarize by list, then click OK**

   The PivotChart report is recalculated to display sales totals. Next, you want to include the total for sales for the Boston store in the Sales sheet by retrieving it from the PivotTable.

4. **Click the Sales sheet tab, click cell G1, type Total Boston Sales:, click the Enter button on the Formula bar, click the Align Right button on the Formatting toolbar, click the Bold button on the Formatting toolbar, then adjust the width of column G to display the label in cell G1**

   You want the GETPIVOTDATA function to retrieve the total Boston sales from the PivotTable.

5. **Click cell H1, type = , click the PivotTable tab, click cell I6 on the PivotTable, then click**

   Cell I6 on the PivotTable contains the data you want to return to the Sales sheet. The GETPIVOTDATA function along with its arguments is inserted into cell H1 of the Sales sheet. Review Figure L-15 for the GETPIVOTDATA arguments.

6. **Click the Currency Style button on the Formatting toolbar**

   The current sales total for the Boston store is $72,989.49, as shown in Figure L-16. This is the same value displayed in cell I6 of the PivotTable.

7. **Enter your name in the Sales sheet footer, save the workbook, then preview and print the Sales worksheet**

8. **Close the file and exit Excel**

FIGURE L-15: Syntax of GETPIVOTDATA function

GETPIVOTDATA("Sales",PivotTable!$A$4, "City", "Boston")

Field where data
is extracted from

PivotTable name and a cell
in the report that contains
the data you want to retrieve

Field and item pair
that describe the data
you want to retrieve

FIGURE L-16: Completed Sales worksheet showing total Boston sales

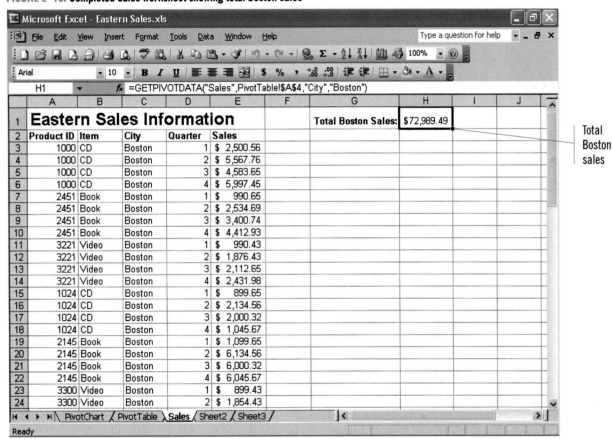

Excel 2003

Total
Boston
sales

Practice

▼ CONCEPTS REVIEW

FIGURE L-17

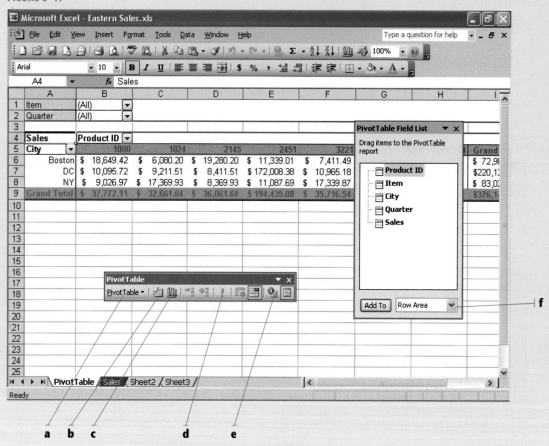

1. Which element do you click to display a list of field settings?
2. Which element do you click to update list changes within a table?
3. Which element do you click to create a PivotChart report?
4. Which element do you click to display a menu of PivotTable commands?
5. Which element do you click to display a list of PivotTable AutoFormats?
6. Which element do you click to display the areas of a PivotTable where fields can be added?

Match each term with the statement that best describes it.

7. **GETPIVOTDATA function**   **a.** Retrieves information from a PivotTable
8. **COLUMN area**   **b.** Displays fields as column labels
9. **Summary function**   **c.** Shows data for one item at a time in a table
10. **PivotTable page**   **d.** Displays values
11. **DATA area**   **e.** Determines if data is summed or averaged

Select the best answer from the list of choices.

12. **Which dialog box allows you to enter a title for a PivotChart?**
    a. PivotChart
    b. PivotTable
    c. Field Items
    d. Chart Options

13. **Which PivotTable report field allows you to average values?**
    a. Data field
    b. Page field
    c. Row field
    d. Column field

14. **To make changes to PivotTable data, you must:**
    a. Create a page field.
    b. Edit cells in the source list and then refresh the PivotTable.
    c. Edit cells in the PivotTable and then refresh the source list.
    d. Drag a column header to the column area.

15. **The PivotTable _____ helps you to create a PivotTable.**
    a. Assistant
    b. Wizard
    c. Designer
    d. Menu

16. **The default summary function for data fields containing numbers in an Excel Pivot table is:**
    a. Average
    b. Sum
    c. Count
    d. Max

17. **A two-dimensional PivotTable can be converted to a three-dimensional PivotTable by adding a:**
    a. Row field
    b. Column field
    c. Page field
    d. Three-dimensional field

18. **Refreshing a PivotTable removes any formatting that was not applied through:**
    a. AutoFormat
    b. PivotTable Format
    c. Format Paragraph
    d. Format Cells

19. **Report formats 1-10 for a PivotTable are _____ formats.**
    a. Database
    b. Indented
    c. Currency
    d. Numerical

20. **The default summary function for data fields containing text in an Excel Pivot table is:**
    a. Min
    b. Max
    c. Count
    d. CountA

▼ SKILLS REVIEW

1. **Plan and design a PivotTable report.**
   a. Start Excel, open the Data File titled EX L-2.xls from the drive and folder where your Data Files are stored, then save it as **July CDs**.
   b. You'll create a PivotTable to show the sum of sales across regions and stores. Study the list, then write down the field names you think should be included in the PivotTable.
   c. Determine which fields you think should be column fields, row fields, and data fields.
   d. Sketch a draft PivotTable.

2. **Create a PivotTable report.**
   a. Open the PivotTable Wizard and create a PivotTable report on a new worksheet using an Excel list.
   b. Add the Product field in the PivotTable List window to the Column Area.
   c. Add the Sales $ field in the PivotTable List window to the Data Area.
   d. Add the Store field in the PivotTable List window to the Row Area.
   e. Add the Sales Rep field in the PivotTable List window to the Row area.
   f. Drag the Store field to the left of the Sales Rep field in the Row Area if necessary.

3. **Change the summary function of a PivotTable report.**
   a. Change the PivotTable summary function to Average using the Field settings button.
   b. Rename the new sheet **July PivotTable**.
   c. Enter your name in the left section of the PivotTable report footer, then save the workbook.
   d. Print the PivotTable report in landscape orientation on one page.
   e. Change the Summary function back to Sum.

4. **Analyze three-dimensional data.**
   a. Add the Region field to the Page Area of the PivotTable.
   b. Display sales for only the West region.
   c. Display sales for all regions.
   d. Display sales for only the East region.
   e. Save the workbook, then print the worksheet.

5. **Update a PivotTable report.**
   a. With the July PivotTable sheet active, note the NY total for Pops Holidays.
   b. Activate the Sales List sheet and change L. Smith's sales of Pops Holidays in cell D8 to **10,843**.
   c. Refresh the PivotTable so it reflects the new sales figure.
   d. Note the NY total for Pops Holidays in the East and verify that it increased by 3000.
   e. Save the workbook, preview then print the PivotTable.

6. **Change the structure and format of a PivotTable report.**
   a. With the July PivotTable active, redisplay data for all regions.
   b. Drag the Product field from the Column Area to the Row Area of the PivotTable.
   c. Drag the Sales Rep field from the Row Area to the Column Area of the PivotTable.
   d. Drag the Store field from the Row Area to the Page Area of the PivotTable.
   e. Remove the Region field from the PivotTable. (*Hint*: To remove a field, drag it back over to the field area in the PivotTable Field list window, or drag it outside the PivotTable area.)
   f. Use the Field Settings button on the PivotTable toolbar to change the numbers to Currency format with no decimal places.
   g. Use the Format Report button on the PivotTable toolbar to apply the Table 4 AutoFormat, save the workbook, then print the PivotTable.

▼ SKILLS REVIEW (CONTINUED)

7. Create a PivotChart report.

    a. Use the existing PivotTable data to create a PivotChart report on a new worksheet.

    b. Rename the chart sheet PivotChart.

    c. Change the chart to display average sales.

    d. Change the chart to display average sales for the LA store only.

    e. Add your name to the left section of the PivotChart sheet footer.

    f. Save the workbook, preview then print the chart.

    g. Change the summary function on the PivotChart sheet back to Sum.

8. Use the GETPIVOTDATA function.

    a. Change the store field on the July PivotTable sheet to show information for all stores.

    b. In cell D26 of the Sales List sheet enter **=**, click the July PivotTable sheet, click the cell that contain the grand total for T. Thomas, then press [Enter].

    c. Review the GETPIVOTDATA function that you entered in cell D26, then format the value as currency with no decimal places.

    d. Enter your name in the Sales List sheet footer, save the workbook, then preview and print the worksheet.

    e. Close the workbook and exit Excel.

▼ INDEPENDENT CHALLENGE 1

You are the bookkeeper for the small accounting firm of Chavez, Long, and Doyle. Until recently, the partners had been tracking their hours manually in a log. You have created an Excel list to track basic information: billing date, partner name, client name, nature of work, and billable hours. It is your responsibility to generate a table summarizing this billing information by client. You will create a PivotTable that sums the hours by partner and date for each project. Once the table is completed, you will create a column chart representing the billing information.

    a. Start Excel, open the Data File titled EX L-3.xls from the drive and folder where your Data Files are stored, then save it as **Partner Billing Report**.

    b. Use the PivotTable Wizard to create a PivotTable on a separate worksheet that sums hours by partner and dates according to client. Use Figure L-18 as a guide.

    c. Name the new sheet **PivotTable** and use the Format Report button on the PivotTable toolbar to apply the Table 3 AutoFormat to the table.

    d. Use the Chart Wizard button on the PivotTable toolbar to create a PivotChart showing the PivotTable information. Name the chart sheet **PivotChart**.

    e. Use the Field Settings button on the PivotTable toolbar to change the summary function in the chart to **Average**.

    f. Add your name to the left section of the PivotTable and PivotChart footers, then save the workbook. Preview and print both the PivotTable and the PivotChart.

    g. Close the workbook and exit Excel.

FIGURE L-18

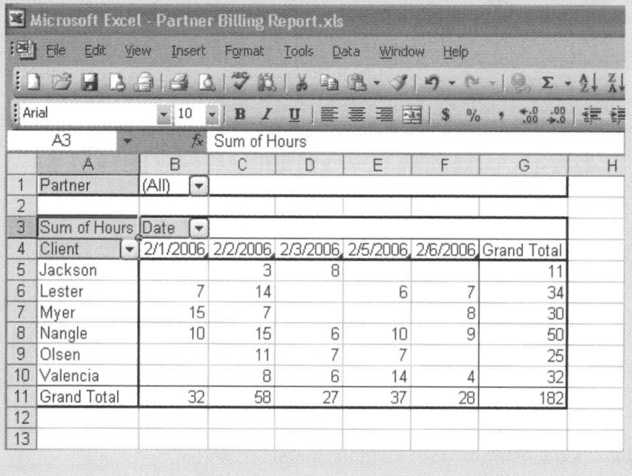

Microsoft Excel - Partner Billing Report.xls

File Edit View Insert Format Tools Data Window Help

Arial 10 | B I U | ≡ ≡ ≡ | $ % , .0 .00 | 律

A3 | fx Sum of Hours

	A	B	C	D	E	F	G	H
1	Partner	(All)						
2								
3	Sum of Hours	Date						
4	Client	2/1/2006	2/2/2006	2/3/2006	2/5/2006	2/6/2006	Grand Total	
5	Jackson		3	8			11	
6	Lester	7	14		6	7	34	
7	Myer	15	7			8	30	
8	Nangle	10	15	6	10	9	50	
9	Olsen		11	7	7		25	
10	Valencia		8	6	14	4	32	
11	Grand Total	32	58	27	37	28	182	
12								
13								

▼ INDEPENDENT CHALLENGE 2

You are the owner of three midsized computer stores called PC Assist. One is located downtown, one is in the Plaza Mall, and one is in the Sun Center shopping center. You have been using Excel to maintain a sales summary list for the second quarter sales in the following three areas: hardware, software, and miscellaneous items. You want to create a PivotTable to analyze and graph the sales in each category by month and store.

a. Start Excel, open the Data File titled EX L-4.xls from the drive and folder where your Data Files are stored, then save it as **Second Qtr Sales**.

b. Rename the Sheet 1 worksheet **Sales**.

c. Create a PivotTable on a new worksheet that sums the sales amount for each store across the rows and each category of sales down the columns. Add a page field for month. Use Figure L-19 as a guide.

d. Change the summary function in the PivotTable to Average.

e. Format the PivotTable using the Table 6 AutoFormat.

f. Format the amounts as Currency with no decimal places.

g. Rename the sheet **PivotTable**.

h. On a separate sheet, create a PivotChart report for the May sales data in all three stores. (*Hint*: Create the PivotChart, then use the Page field list arrow to select May.) Name the chart sheet **PivotChart**.

i. Add a descriptive title to your chart, using the Chart Options dialog box.

j. Add your name to the left section of the PivotTable and PivotChart worksheet footers, save the workbook, then print the PivotTable and the PivotChart.

k. Close the workbook and exit Excel.

FIGURE L-19

	A	B	C	D	E
1	Month	(All)			
2					
3	Sum of Amount	Category			
4	Store	Hardware	Misc	Software	Grand Total
5	Downtown	140236	24139	70340	234715
6	Plaza Mall	141331	19233	62880	223444
7	Sun Center	124233	21300	57895	203428
8	Grand Total	405800	64672	191115	661587

▼ INDEPENDENT CHALLENGE 3

You manage a group of sales offices in the Western region for a cellular phone company called Digital West. Management has asked you to provide a summary table showing information on your sales staff, including their locations and their titles. You have been using Excel to keep track of the staff in the San Francisco, Phoenix, and Portland offices. Now you will create a PivotTable and PivotChart summarizing this information.

a. Start Excel, open the Data File titled EX L-5.xls from the drive and folder where your Data Files are stored, then save it as **Western Sales Employees**.

b. Create a PivotTable on a new worksheet that lists the number of employees in each city, with the names of the cities listed across the columns and the titles listed down the rows. (*Hint*: Remember that the default summary function for cells containing text is Count.) Use Figure L-20 as a guide.

c. Rename the new sheet **PivotTable**.

d. Create a PivotChart using the PivotTable information that shows the number of employees in each store by position. Rename the new chart sheet **PivotChart**.

e. Add a chart title of **Western Sales Staff**.

f. Insert a new row in the Employee List worksheet above row 7. In the new row, add information reflecting the recent hiring of Cathy Connolly, a sales manager, at the Phoenix office. Update the PivotTable to display the new employee information.

FIGURE L-20

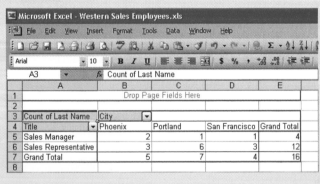

	A	B	C	D	E
1		Drop Page Fields Here			
2					
3	Count of Last Name	City			
4	Title	Phoenix	Portland	San Francisco	Grand Total
5	Sales Manager	2	1	1	4
6	Sales Representative	3	6	3	12
7	Grand Total	5	7	4	16
8					

▼ INDEPENDENT CHALLENGE 3 (CONTINUED)

g. Add the label **Total Phoenix Staff:** in cell C20 of the Employee List sheet. Right-align and boldface the label in cell C20.

h. Enter a function in cell D20 that retrieves the total number of employees located in Phoenix from the PivotTable.

Advanced Challenge Exercise

- Rename the Title field name on the PivotTable to **Position**.
- Rename the Count of Last Name field to **Number of Employees**.
- Check the PivotChart to be sure that the new field names have been added.

i. Add your name to the left section of all three worksheet footers, save the workbook, then print the PivotTable, the Employee List, and the PivotChart.

j. Close the workbook and exit Excel.

▼ INDEPENDENT CHALLENGE 4

You are a member of an investment group that meets weekly on Thursday evenings. You need to prepare a report for this week's meeting showing the performance of three stocks over the past five business days. You decide to use a PivotTable and a PivotChart to represent the market trends for the stocks you are researching. You will begin by researching stock prices on the Web and charting each stock for the past five business days. Then you will use a PivotTable function to display each stock's weekly high. Last, you will use a PivotChart to represent each stock's five-day performance.

a. Start Excel, create a new workbook, then save it as **Stock Prices** in the drive and folder where your Data Files are stored.

b. Use the search engine of your choice to research stock prices. (*Hint*: You may want to enter **stock price history** as your search fields. If your search engine requires a + sign between fields be sure to enter them also.)

c. Record prices for three stocks of your choice over the past five days, then create a list that contains your stock research data. Name the list worksheet **Price**. Use Figure L-21 as a guide.

d. Create a PivotTable on a new worksheet that sums the stock prices for each stock across the rows and each day down the columns. Rename the PivotTable sheet **PivotTable**.

e. Format the sales figures as currency with two decimal places and apply the Table 6 AutoFormat.

f. Change the summary function in the PivotTable to **MAX** to show the highest stock price.

g. Create a PivotChart report from your data on a separate sheet. Change the Column chart to a Bar chart. (*Hint*: Use the Chart Type dialog box). Rename the sheet **PivotChart**.

h. Enter the label **Highest Price** in cell F1 of the Price sheet. Right-align and bold-face the label in cell F1.

i. Enter a function in cell G1 that retrieves the highest price for one of your stocks over the past five days from the PivotTable. Add the stock name to the label in cell F1.

FIGURE L-21

	A	B	C	D
1	Stock	Day	Price	
2	Stock 1	1		
3	Stock 1	2		
4	Stock 1	3		
5	Stock 1	4		
6	Stock 1	5		
7	Stock 2	1		
8	Stock 2	2		
9	Stock 2	3		
10	Stock 2	4		
11	Stock 2	5		
12	Stock 3	1		
13	Stock 3	2		
14	Stock 3	3		
15	Stock 3	4		
16	Stock 3	5		

Advanced Challenge Exercise

- Change the structure of the PivotTable, moving the Day field to the Row Area and Stock to the Column Area. Verify that the highest price for a stock is still correct on the Price worksheet.
- Move the stock information in the first column of the PivotTable to the last column.
- Change the Grand Total label in cell A10 of the PivotTable to **Highest Price**.

j. Add your name to the left section of each worksheet footer, save the workbook, then print the PivotTable, the Price sheet, and the PivotChart.

k. Close the workbook and exit Excel.

Excel 2003

▼ VISUAL WORKSHOP

Open the workbook titled EX L-6.xls from the drive and folder where your Data Files are stored, then save it as **Photo Store**. Using the data in the workbook, create the PivotTable shown in Figure L-22. (*Hint*: There are two data summary fields and the table has been formatted using the Table 4 AutoFormat.) Add your name to the PivotTable sheet footer, then preview and print the PivotTable. Save the worksheet, then close the workbook.

FIGURE L-22

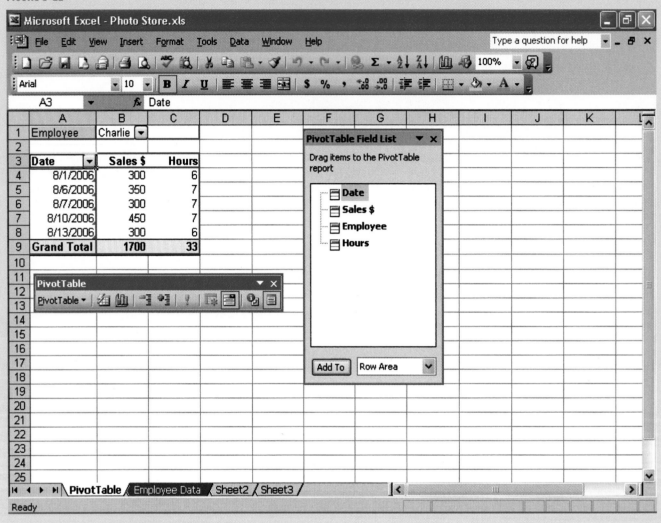

UNIT M
Excel 2003

Exchanging Data with Other Programs

OBJECTIVES

Plan a data exchange	
Import a text file	
Import a database table	
Insert a graphic file in a worksheet	
Embed a worksheet	
Link a worksheet to another program	
Embed an Excel chart into a PowerPoint slide	
Import a list into an Access table	

If you have a SAM user profile, you may have access to hands-on instruction, practice, and assessment of the skills covered in this unit. Log in to your SAM account and go to your assignments page to see what your instructor has assigned.

In a Windows environment, you can freely exchange data among Excel and most other Windows programs, a process known as **integration**. In this unit, you will plan a data exchange between Excel and other Microsoft Office programs. ░░░░ MediaLoft's upper management has asked Jim Fernandez, the marketing director, to research the possible purchase of CafeCorp, a small company that operates cafés in large businesses, hospitals, and, more recently, drug stores. Jim is reviewing the broker's paper documents and electronic files and developing a presentation on the feasibility of acquiring this company. To complete this project, Jim asks you to help set up the exchange of data between Excel and other programs.

Planning a Data Exchange

Because the tools available in Microsoft Office programs are designed to be compatible, exchanging data between Excel and other programs is easy. The first step involves planning what you want to accomplish with each data exchange.  Jim asks you to use the following guidelines to plan data exchanges between Excel and other programs in order to complete the business analysis project.

To plan an exchange of data:

- **Identify the data you want to exchange, its file type, and, if possible, the program used to create it**

  Whether the data you want to exchange is a graphics file, a database file, a worksheet, or consists only of text, it is important to identify the data's **source program** (the program used to create it) and the file type. Once you identify the source program, you can determine options for exchanging that data with Excel. Jim needs to analyze a text file containing the CafeCorp product data. Although he does not know the source program, Jim knows that the file contains unformatted text. A file that consists of text but no formatting is sometimes called an **ASCII** or **text** file. Because ASCII is a universally accepted file format, Jim can easily import an ASCII file into Excel. See Table M-1 for a partial list of other file formats that Excel can import. For more information on importable file formats, see the Help topic "File format converters supplied with Excel".

- **Determine the program with which you want to exchange data**

  Besides knowing which program created the data you want to exchange, you must also identify which program will receive the data, called the **destination program**. This determines the procedure you use to perform the exchange. You might want to insert a graphic object into an Excel worksheet or add a spreadsheet to a Word document. Jim received a database table of CafeCorp's corporate customers created with the Access database program. After determining that Excel can import Access tables and reviewing the import procedure, he imports that database file into Excel so he can analyze it using Excel tools.

- **Determine the goal of your data exchange**

  Although it is convenient to use the Office Clipboard to cut, copy, and paste data within and between programs, you cannot retain a connection with the source program when using these methods. However, there are two ways to transfer data within and between programs that allow you to retain some connection with the source program. These data transfer methods use a Windows feature known as **object linking and embedding**, or **OLE**. The data to be exchanged, called an **object**, may consist of text, a worksheet, or any other type of data. You use **embedding** to insert a copy of the original object in the destination document and, if necessary, to subsequently edit this data separately from the source document. This process is illustrated in Figure M-1. You use **linking** when you want the information you inserted to be updated automatically when the data in the source document changes. This process is illustrated in Figure M-2. Embedding and linking are discussed in more detail later in this unit. Jim has determined that he needs to use both object embedding and object linking for his analysis and presentation project.

- **Set up the data exchange**

  When you exchange data between two programs, it is often best to start both programs prior to starting the exchange. You might also want to tile the program windows on the screen either horizontally or vertically so that you can see both during the exchange. You will work with Excel, Word, Access, and PowerPoint when exchanging data for this project.

- **Execute the data exchange**

  The steps you use will vary, depending on the type of data you want to exchange. Jim is ready to have you start the data exchanges for the business analysis of CafeCorp.

FIGURE M-1: Embedded object

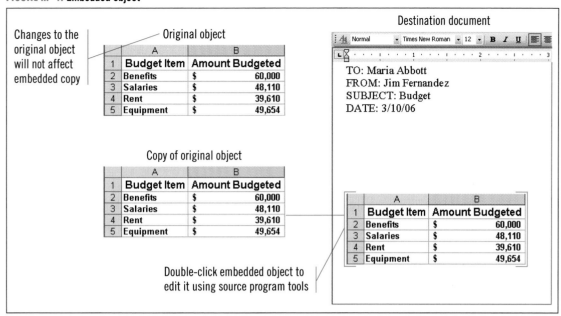

Changes to the original object will not affect embedded copy

Original object

Copy of original object

Double-click embedded object to edit it using source program tools

FIGURE M-2: Linked object

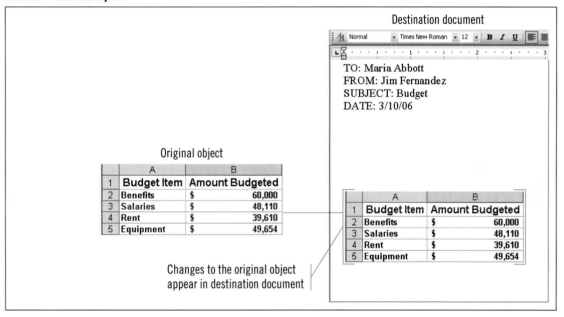

Original object

Changes to the original object appear in destination document

TABLE M-1: Importable file formats and extensions

file format	file extension(s)	file format	file extension(s)
dBASE 2,3,4	.dbf	CSV (comma separated values)	.csv
Excel 97–XP	.xls, .xlt (template), .xlw (workspace)	DIF (Data Interchange Format)	.dif
Quattro/Quattro Pro	.wq1, .wb1, .wb3	Formatted text (Space or column delimited)	.txt, .prn
Lotus 1-2-3	.wks, .wk1, .wk3, .wk4	Text (Tab delimited)	.txt
HTML	.htm	XML	.xml
Web page	.mht	SYLK (Symbolic Link)	.slk
Microsoft Works	.wks		

Importing a Text File

You can import data created in other programs into Excel by opening the file, as long as Excel can read the file type. After importing the file, you use the Save As command on the File menu to save the data in Excel format. Text files use a tab or space as the **delimiter**, or column separator, to separate columns of data. When you import a text file into Excel, the Text Import Wizard automatically opens and describes how text is separated in the imported file. ▓▓▓ Now that Jim has planned the data exchange, he wants you to import a tab-delimited text file containing product cost and pricing data from CafeCorp.

STEPS

1. **Start Excel if necessary, click the** Open button ⬚ **on the Standard toolbar, click the** Look in list arrow, **then navigate to the folder containing your Data Files**

   The Open dialog box shows only those files that match the file types listed in the Files of type box—usually Microsoft Excel files. In this case, however, you're importing a text file.

TROUBLE

In the Preview window, small squares may separate the field. You can continue with the lesson.

2. **Click the** Files of type list arrow, **click** Text Files, **click** EX M-1.txt, **then click** Open

   The first Text Import Wizard dialog box opens. See Figure M-3. Under Original data type, the Delimited option button is selected. In the Preview of file box, line 1 indicates that the file contains three columns of data: Item, Cost, and Price. No changes are necessary in this dialog box.

3. **Click** Next

   The second Text Import Wizard dialog box opens. Under Delimiters, Tab is selected as the delimiter, indicating that tabs separate the columns of incoming data. The Data preview box contains lines showing where the tab delimiters divide the data into columns.

4. **Click** Next

   The third Text Import Wizard dialog box opens with options for formatting the three columns of data. Under Column data format, the General option button is selected. This is the best formatting option for text mixed with numbers.

5. **Click** Finish

   Excel imports the text file into the blank worksheet as three columns of data: Item, Cost, and Price.

QUICK TIP

If you do not specify Excel as the file type, you will be asked if you want to proceed. Click No, then choose Excel in the Save as type list box.

6. **Maximize the Excel window if necessary, click** File **on the menu bar, click** Save As, **make sure the folder containing your Data Files appears in the Save in box, click the** Save as type list arrow, **scroll up and click** Microsoft Office Excel Workbook (*.xls), **change the filename to** CafeCorp, **then click** Save

   The file is saved as an Excel workbook, and the new name appears in the title bar. The sheet tab automatically changes to the name of the imported file, EX M-1. The worksheet information would be easier to read if it were formatted and if it showed the profit for each item.

7. **Double-click the border between the headers in** Columns A **and** B, **click cell** D1, **type** Profit, **click cell** D2, **type** =, **click cell** C2, **type** -, **click cell** B2, **click the** Enter button ☑ **on the Formula bar, then copy the formula in cell** D2 **to the range** D3:D18

8. **Rename the sheet tab** Product Information, **center the column labels, apply bold formatting to them, format the data in columns B, C, and D using the Number style with two decimal places, then click cell** A1

   Figure M-4 shows the completed worksheet, which analyzes the text file data you imported into Excel.

9. **Add your name to the left section of the worksheet footer, save the workbook, preview and print the worksheet, then close the workbook**

FIGURE M-3: First Text Import Wizard dialog box

Original data type is delimited

Three column headings

Preview of file contents

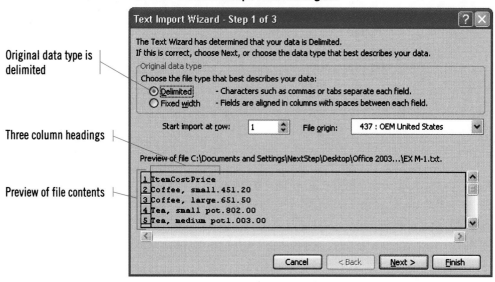

FIGURE M-4: Completed worksheet with imported text file

Columns from text file

Added column with new profit data

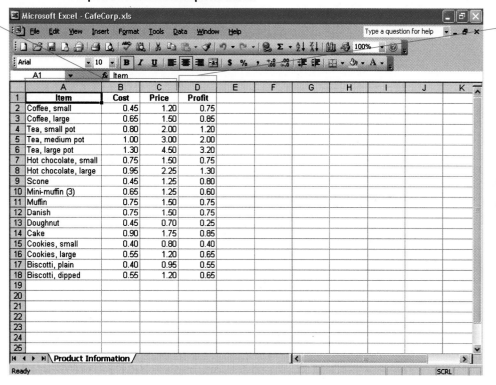

Clues to Use

Other ways to import files

Another way to open the Text Import Wizard is by pointing to Import External Data on the Data menu, clicking Import Data, then selecting a data source. Although the Text Import Wizard gives you the most flexibility, there are other ways to import text files. For example, on the Windows desktop, you can drag the icon representing a text file into a blank worksheet window, and Excel will create a worksheet from the data without going through the wizard.

Importing a Database Table

In addition to importing text files, you can also use Excel to import files from other programs or from database tables. To import files that contain importable file formats, open the file in Excel, then work with the data and save it as an Excel workbook. ▓▓▓▓▓ Jim received a database table containing CafeCorp's corporate customers, which was created with Access. He asks you to import this table into the workbook, then format, sort, and total the data.

STEPS

1. **Click the** New button ▢ **on the Standard toolbar**
   A new workbook opens, displaying a blank worksheet to which you can import the Access data.

2. **Click** Data **on the menu bar, point to** Import External Data, **click** Import Data, **then click the** Look in list arrow **and navigate to the folder containing your Data Files**

QUICK TIP
You can move the External Data toolbar if you can't see your worksheet data.

3. **Make sure** All Data Sources **appears in the Files of type text box, click** EX M-2.mdb, **click** Open, **then click** OK **in the Import Data dialog box**
   Excel inserts the Access data into the worksheet starting in cell A1 and displays the External Data toolbar. See Figure M-5.

4. **Rename the sheet tab** Customer Information, **then format the data in** columns F **and** G **with the Number format, using commas and no decimal places**
   You are ready to sort the data in columns F and G.

5. **Click cell** G1, **then click the** Sort Descending button ▤ **on the Standard toolbar**
   The records are reorganized in descending order according to the amount of the 2006 orders.

6. **Select the range** F19:G19, **click the** AutoSum button Σ **on the Standard toolbar, then return to cell A1**
   Your completed worksheet should match Figure M-6.

7. **Add your name to the left section of the worksheet footer, save the workbook as** Customer Information, **then preview and print the worksheet in landscape orientation**

Clues to Use

Using smart tags

When Excel recognizes certain data types, it marks the cell with a smart tag, a small, purple triangle in the lower-right corner of the cell. For example, if you type a name that matches a name in an Outlook address book, you can use the smart tag to send an e-mail to that person from within Excel. To see a list of what actions you can take, point to the smart tag, then click the Smart Tag Actions button ⊕ that appears. To turn smart tags on or off, click Tools on the menu bar, click AutoCorrect Options, click the Smart Tags tab, then select or deselect "Label data with smart tags."

FIGURE M-5: Imported Access table

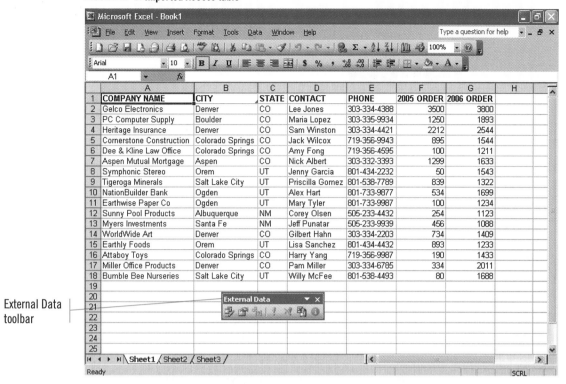

External Data toolbar

FIGURE M-6: Completed worksheet containing imported data

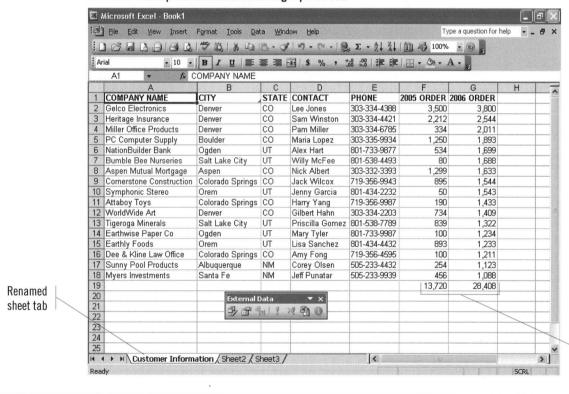

Renamed sheet tab

Totals added to columns F and G

Clues to Use

Exporting cell data

Most of the file types that Excel can import (listed in Table M-1) are also the file types which Excel can export, or deliver data. Excel can also export HTML and XML formats for the Web. To export an Excel worksheet, use the Save As command on the File menu, click the Save as type list arrow, then select the desired format. Saving in a non-Excel format might result in the loss of formatting that is unique to Excel.

Inserting a Graphic File in a Worksheet

A graphic object (such as a drawing, logo, or photograph) can greatly enhance a worksheet's visual impact. The Picture options on the Insert menu make it easy to insert graphics into an Excel worksheet. Once you've inserted a picture, you can format it using the tools on the Picture toolbar. **█████** Jim wants you to insert the upper part of the MediaLoft logo at the top of the customer worksheet. The company's Marketing Department has created the graphic and saved it in JPG format. You insert and format the image on the worksheet. You start by creating a space for the logo on the worksheet.

STEPS

1. **Select rows 1 through 5, click Insert on the menu bar, then click Rows**
   Five blank rows appear above the header row, leaving space to insert the picture.

2. **Click cell A1, click Insert on the menu bar, then point to Picture**
   The Picture submenu opens. See Figure M-7. This menu offers several options for inserting graphics. You want to insert a picture that you already have in a file. The file you will insert has a .jpg file extension, so it is called a "jay-peg" file. JPEG files can be viewed in a Web browser.

   TROUBLE
   If the picture toolbar is not displayed, right-click any toolbar, then click Picture from the shortcut menu.

3. **Click From File, make sure the folder containing your Data Files appears in the Look in box, click EX M-3.jpg, then click Insert**
   Excel inserts the graphic and opens the Picture toolbar. The small circles around the picture's border are sizing handles. Sizing handles appear when a picture is selected; you use them to change the size of a picture.

4. **Position the pointer over the sizing handle in the logo's lower-right corner, drag the corner up and to the left so that the logo's outline fits within rows 1 through 5**
   Compare your screen to Figure M-8. You will lower the picture's contrast and brightness.

   QUICK TIP
   You can rotate a picture using the Rotate Left 90° button on the Picture toolbar. For more rotating options, click the Format Picture button on the Picture toolbar, then click the Size tab and enter a value in the Rotation textbox.

5. **With the picture image selected, click the Less Contrast button on the Picture toolbar three times, then click the Less Brightness button**
   You will crop the image to remove the text at the bottom.

6. **Click the Crop button on the Picture toolbar, then drag the bottom-center cropping handle up to crop out the MediaLoft text**
   The logo will look better on the worksheet without the blue background.

7. **Click the Set Transparent Color button on the Picture toolbar, then click anywhere on the blue background of the logo**

8. **Save the workbook, preview then print the worksheet, close the workbook, then exit Excel**
   Your completed worksheet should match Figure M-9.

Clues to Use

Importing data from HTML files

You can import information from HTML files and Web pages into Excel by using drag and drop or the Insert Object command. To use drag and drop, open Internet Explorer, then open the HTML file or Web page that contains the data you want to import. Resize the Explorer window so it covers only half of the screen. Open the Excel file to which you want to import the data, then resize the Excel window so it covers the other half of the screen. In the Explorer window, highlight the table or information you want to import, then drag it over to the Excel window. When the pointer changes to the Copy Pointer, release the mouse button. The information will appear in your Excel document, ready for analysis. You can also open an HTML file from your intranet or a Web site in Excel and modify it. To retrieve data from a particular Web page on a regular basis, use a Web query, which you'll learn about in the next unit.

FIGURE M-7: Picture menu

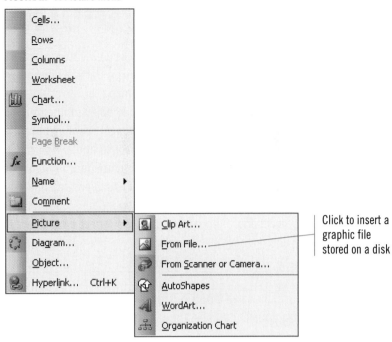

Cells...
Rows
Columns
Worksheet
Chart...
Symbol...
Page Break
Function...
Name ▶
Comment
Picture ▶
Diagram...
Object...
Hyperlink... Ctrl+K

Clip Art...
From File...
From Scanner or Camera...
AutoShapes
WordArt...
Organization Chart

Click to insert a
graphic file
stored on a disk

FIGURE M-8: Picture toolbar

Less
Brightness
button

Less Contrast
button

Sizing handle

Crop button

Set
Transparent
Color button

FIGURE M-9: Worksheet with formatted picture

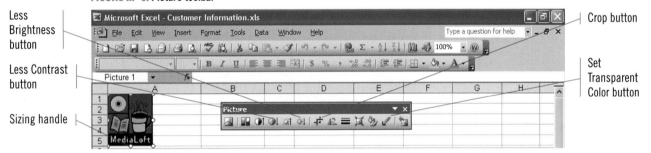

Formatted
picture

	A	B	C	D	E	F	G
6	COMPANY NAME	CITY	STATE	CONTACT	PHONE	2005 ORDER	2006 ORDER
7	Gelco Electronics	Denver	CO	Lee Jones	303-334-4388	3,500	3,800
8	Heritage Insurance	Denver	CO	Sam Winston	303-334-4421	2,212	2,544
9	Miller Office Products	Denver	CO	Pam Miller	303-334-6785	334	2,011
10	PC Computer Supply	Boulder	CO	Maria Lopez	303-335-9934	1,250	1,893
11	NationBuilder Bank	Ogden	UT	Alex Hart	801-733-9877	534	1,699
12	Bumble Bee Nurseries	Salt Lake City	UT	Willy McFee	801-538-4493	80	1,688
13	Aspen Mutual Mortgage	Aspen	CO	Nick Albert	303-332-3393	1,299	1,633
14	Cornerstone Construction	Colorado Springs	CO	Jack Wilcox	719-356-9943	895	1,544
15	Symphonic Stereo	Orem	UT	Jenny Garcia	801-434-2232	50	1,543
16	Attaboy Toys	Colorado Springs	CO	Harry Yang	719-356-9987	190	1,433
17	WorldWide Art	Denver	CO	Gilbert Hahn	303-334-2203	734	1,409
18	Tigeroga Minerals	Salt Lake City	UT	Priscilla Gomez	801-538-7789	839	1,322
19	Earthwise Paper Co	Ogden	UT	Mary Tyler	801-733-9987	100	1,234
20	Earthly Foods	Orem	UT	Lisa Sanchez	801-434-4432	893	1,233
21	Dee & Kline Law Office	Colorado Springs	CO	Amy Fong	719-356-4595	100	1,211
22	Sunny Pool Products	Albuquerque	NM	Corey Olsen	505-233-4432	254	1,123
23	Myers Investments	Santa Fe	NM	Jeff Punatar	505-233-9939	456	1,088
24						13,720	28,408

Embedding a Worksheet

Microsoft Office programs work together to make it easy to copy an object (such as text, data, or a graphic) in a source program and then insert it into a document in a different program (the destination program). If you insert the object using a simple Paste command, however, you retain no connection to the source program. That's why it is often more useful to embed objects rather than simply paste them. Embedding allows you to edit an Excel workbook from within a different program using Excel commands and tools. If you send a Word document with an embedded worksheet to another person, you do not need to send a separate Excel file with it. All the necessary information is embedded in the Word document. When you embed information, you can either display the data itself, or an icon representing the data; users double-click the icon to view the embedded data. 📇 Jim decides to update Maria on the project status. He asks you to prepare a Word memo, including the projected sales worksheet embedded as an icon. You begin by starting the Word program and opening the memo.

STEPS

1. **Start Word, click the Open button** 📄 **on the Standard toolbar, make sure the folder containing your Data Files appears in the Look in box, click EX M-4.doc, then click Open**
   The memo opens in Word.

2. **Click File on the menu bar, click Save As, make sure the folder containing your Data Files appears in the Save in box, change the file name to CafeCorp Sales Memo, then click Save**
   You want to embed the worksheet below the last line of the document.

> **QUICK TIP**
> You can also use the Object dialog box to embed an HTML file in an Excel worksheet.

3. **Press [Ctrl][End], click Insert on the menu bar, click Object, then click the Create from File tab in the Object dialog box**
   See Figure M-10. You need to indicate the file you want to embed.

4. **Click Browse, make sure the folder containing your Data Files appears in the Look in box, click EX M-5.xls, click Insert, select the Display as icon check box**
   You will change the icon to a more descriptive name.

> **QUICK TIP**
> To display a different icon to represent the file, scroll down the icon list and select any icon.

5. **Click the Change Icon button, delete the text in the Caption textbox and type Projected Sales, then click OK twice**
   The memo contains an embedded copy of the sales projection worksheet, displayed as an icon. See Figure M-11.

6. **Double-click the Projected Sales worksheet icon on the Word memo then maximize the Excel window and the worksheet window if necessary**
   The Excel program starts and displays the embedded worksheet, with its location displayed in the title bar. See Figure M-12. Any changes you make to the embedded object using Excel tools are not reflected in the source document. Similarly, if you open the source document in the source program, changes you make are not reflected in the embedded copy.

7. **Click File on the Excel menu bar, click Close & Return to CafeCorp Sales Memo.doc, close Excel, then click the Save button** 💾 **on the Word toolbar to save the memo**

FIGURE M-10: Object dialog box

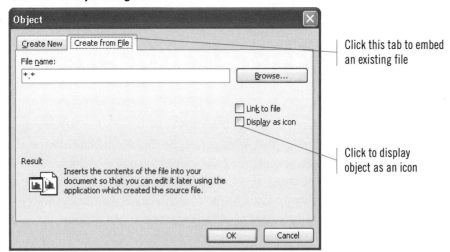

Click this tab to embed an existing file

Click to display object as an icon

FIGURE M-11: Memo with embedded worksheet

Memo is a Word document

Icon representing the embedded Excel worksheet

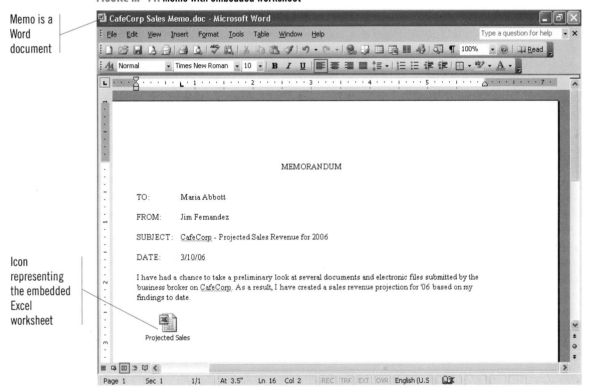

FIGURE M-12: Embedded worksheet opened in Excel

Location of the embedded worksheet

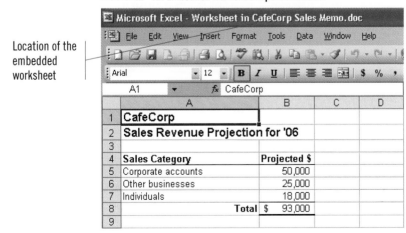

Excel 2003

Linking a Worksheet to Another Program

Linking a worksheet into another program retains a connection with the original document as well as the original program. When you link a worksheet to another program, the link contains a connection to the source document so that, when you double-click it, the source document opens for editing. Once you link a worksheet to another program, any changes you make to the original worksheet (the source document) are reflected in the linked object. ▓▓▓ Jim realizes he may be making some changes to the workbook he embedded in the memo to Maria. To ensure that these changes will be reflected in the memo, he feels you should use linking instead of embedding. He asks you to delete the embedded worksheet icon and replace it with a linked version of the same worksheet.

STEPS

1. **With the Word memo still open, click the Microsoft Excel Worksheet icon to select it if necessary, then press [Delete]**

   The embedded worksheet is removed. The linking process is similar to embedding.

2. **Make sure the insertion point is below the last line of the memo, click Insert on the Word menu bar, click Object, then click the Create from File tab in the Object dialog box**

QUICK TIP

If you want to insert part of an existing worksheet into another file, you can copy the information that you want to link and then use the Paste Special option on the Edit menu to paste a link to the source file.

3. **Click Browse, make sure the folder containing your Data Files appears in the Look in box, click EX M-5.xls, click Insert, select the Link to file check box, then click OK**

   The memo now displays a linked copy of the sales projection worksheet. See Figure M-13. In the future, any changes made to the source file, EX M-5, will also be made to the linked copy in the Word memo. You verify this by making a change to the source file and viewing its effect on the Word memo.

4. **Click the Save button 🖫 on the Standard toolbar, then close the Word memo and exit Word**

   The sales projection for other businesses has changed to $20,000.

5. **Start Excel, open the file EX M-5.xls from the drive and folder where your Data Files are stored, click cell B6, type 20,000, then press [Enter]**

   You want to verify that the same change was made automatically to the linked copy of the worksheet.

6. **Start Word, open CafeCorp Sales Memo from the drive and folder where your Data Files are stored, then click Yes if asked if you want to update the document's links**

   The memo displays the new value in cell B6 and an updated total. See Figure M-14.

7. **Click View on the menu bar, click Header and Footer, type your name in the header box, then click Close on the Header and Footer toolbar**

8. **Save the Word memo, preview and print it, then close it and exit Word**

9. **Close the Excel worksheet without saving it, then exit Excel**

FIGURE M-13: Memo with linked worksheet

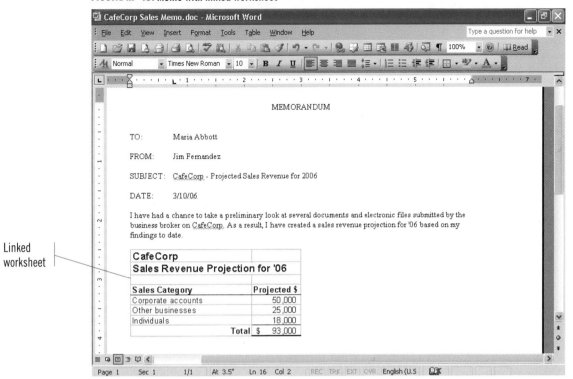

Linked
worksheet

FIGURE M-14: Memo with link updated

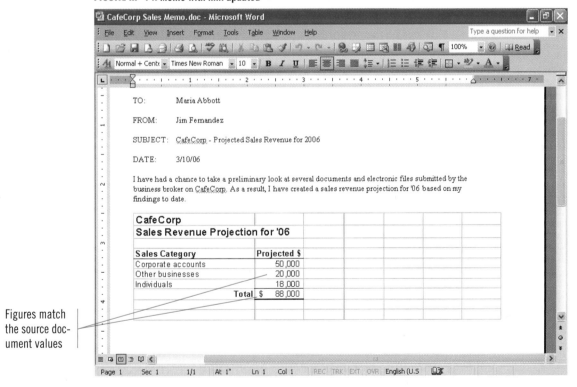

Figures match
the source doc-
ument values

Clues to Use

Managing links

When you change a source file, the link is updated automatically each time you open the destination document. You can manage linked objects further by choosing Links on the Edit menu. This opens the Links dialog box, which allows you to update a link or to change the source file of a link. You can also break a link by selecting the source file in the Links dialog box and clicking Break Link.

Embedding an Excel Chart into a PowerPoint Slide

Microsoft PowerPoint is a **presentation graphics** program that you can use to create slide show presentations. For example, you could create a slide show to present a sales plan to management or to inform potential clients about a new service. PowerPoint slides can include a mix of text, data, and graphics. Adding an Excel chart to a slide can help to illustrate data and give your presentation more visual appeal.  Upper management asks Jim to brief the Marketing Department on the possible acquisition of CafeCorp, based on his analysis so far. Jim will make his presentation using PowerPoint slides. He decides to add an Excel chart to one of the presentation slides, illustrating the 2006 sales projection data. He begins by starting PowerPoint.

STEPS

1. **Click the Start button on the task bar, point to All Programs, point to Microsoft Office, click Microsoft Office PowerPoint 2003, click the More button 🖙 in the Open section of the Getting Started task pane, make sure the folder containing your Data Files appears in the Look in box, click EX M-6.ppt, then click Open**

   The presentation appears in Normal view and contains three panes and the Drawing toolbar, as shown in Figure M-15.

2. **Click File on the menu bar, click Save As, make sure the folder containing your Data Files appears in the Save in box, change the file name to Marketing Department Presentation, then click Save**

   The outline of the presentation in the Outline pane on the left shows the title and text for each slide. You will add an Excel chart to Slide 2, "2006 Sales Projections." To add the chart, you first need to select the slide on which it will appear.

3. **Click the Slide 2 icon ▦ in the Outline pane**

   The slide appears in the Slide pane on the right.

4. **Click Insert on the menu bar, then click Object**

   The Insert Object dialog box opens. You want to insert an object (the Excel chart) that has already been saved as a file.

5. **Click the Create from file option button, click Browse, click the Look in list arrow, navigate to the folder containing your Data Files, click EX M-7.xls, click OK, then in the Insert Object dialog box click OK again**

   After a moment, a pie chart illustrating the 2006 sales projections appears in the slide with resizing handles. The chart would look better if it was larger.

QUICK TIP
If you need to move the selected chart to center it, you can use the arrow keys on the keyboard.

6. **Drag the lower-right corner sizing handle down and to the right to increase the chart size, then press [Esc] to deselect the chart**

   Slide Show view displays the slide on the full screen the way the audience will see it.

7. **Click the Slide Show from current slide button 🖵 in the lower-left corner of the screen**

   The finished sales projection slide appears, as shown in Figure M-16. The presentation for the Marketing Department is complete.

8. **Press [Esc] to return to Normal view, in the Outline pane click at the end of the Slide 2 text: "2006 Sales Projections"; press [Spacebar], type by followed by your name, then click the Save button 🖫 on the PowerPoint Standard toolbar**

9. **Click File on the menu bar, click Print, under Print Range select the Current slide option, click OK, close the presentation, then exit PowerPoint**

FIGURE M-15: Presentation in Normal view

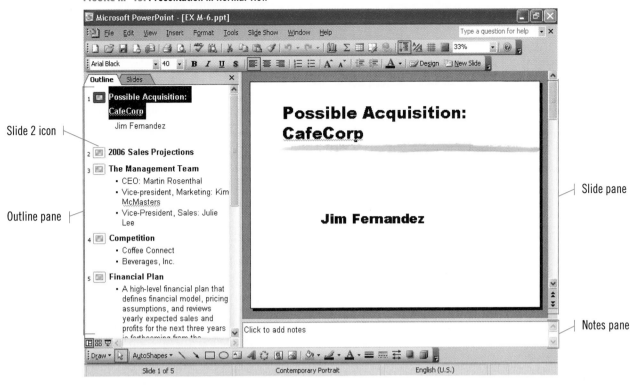

Slide 2 icon

Outline pane

Slide pane

Notes pane

FIGURE M-16: Completed Sales Projections slide in Slide Show view

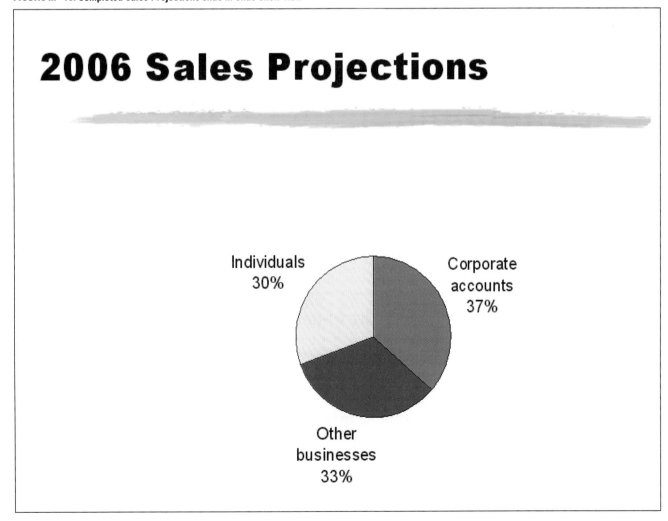

UNIT
M
Excel 2003

Importing a List into an Access Table

If you need to analyze an Excel list using the more extensive tools of a database, you can import the list into Microsoft Access, a database program. Column labels in Excel become field names in Access. Once converted to Access format, a data list is called a **table**. In the process of importing an Excel list, Access specifies a primary key for the new table. A **primary key** is the field that contains unique information for each record (row) of information. ▓▓▓▓ Jim has just received a workbook containing salary information for the managers at CafeCorp. He asks you to convert the list to a Microsoft Access table.

STEPS

1. **Click the** Start button **on the task bar, point to** All Programs, **point to** Microsoft Office, **click** Microsoft Office Access 2003, **click** Create a new file **in the Getting Started task pane, then click** Blank database **in the task pane**

2. **Click the** Save in list arrow, **navigate to the disk and folder containing your Data Files, change the filename in the File name text box to** CafeCorp Management, **then click** Create

   The database window for the CafeCorp Management database opens. You are ready to import the Excel list.

> **QUICK TIP**
> You can also use the Microsoft AccessLinks Add-in program, available on the Web, to convert an Excel list to an Access table from within Excel.

3. **Click** File **on the menu bar, point to** Get External Data, **click** Import, **make sure the folder containing your Data Files appears in the Look in box, select** Microsoft Excel (*.xls) **in the Files of type box, click** EX M-8.xls, **then click** Import

   The First Import Spreadsheet Wizard dialog box opens. See Figure M-17. The top section of the dialog box shows the sheets in the workbook. The Compensation worksheet is selected by default, and a sample of the sheet data appears in the lower section. In the next dialog box, you indicate that you want to use the column headings in the Excel list as the field names in the Access database.

4. **Click** Next, **make sure the** First Row Contains Column Headings check box **is selected, then click** Next

   You want to store the Excel data in a new table.

5. **Make sure the** In a New Table option button **is selected, then click** Next

   The wizard has converted the column headings from the Excel list into field names. Your completed Import Spreadsheet Wizard dialog box should match Figure M-18. The table's primary key field contains unique information for each record; the Employee field is unique for each person in the list.

> **QUICK TIP**
> Specifying a primary key allows you to retrieve data more quickly in the future.

6. **Click** Next, **select the** Choose my own primary key option, **make sure Employee Number appears in the list box next to the selected option button, click** Next, **click** Finish, **then click** OK

   The icon and name of the new Access table ("Compensation") appears in the database window.

7. **Make sure that** Compensation **is selected, click** Open **in the Database toolbar, then maximize the table window**

   The data from the Excel worksheet is displayed in a new Access table. See Figure M-19.

8. **Double-click the border between the Employee Number and First Name column headings, then use the last row of the table to enter** your name **in the First Name and Last Name columns and enter** 0 **for an Employee Number**

9. **Click the** Save button 🔲 **on the Table Datasheet toolbar, click the** Print button 🖨 **on the Table Datasheet toolbar to print the table, close the table, then exit Access**

FIGURE M-17: First Import Spreadsheet Wizard dialog box

Excel data to be imported

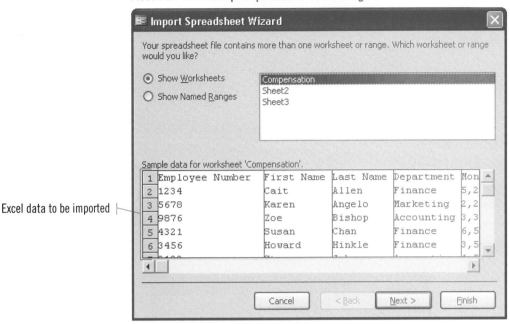

FIGURE M-18: Completed Import Spreadsheet Wizard dialog box

Field names

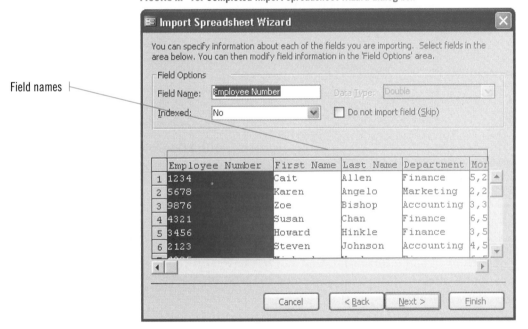

FIGURE M-19: Completed Access table

Primary key

Access table

Practice

▼ CONCEPTS REVIEW

FIGURE M-20

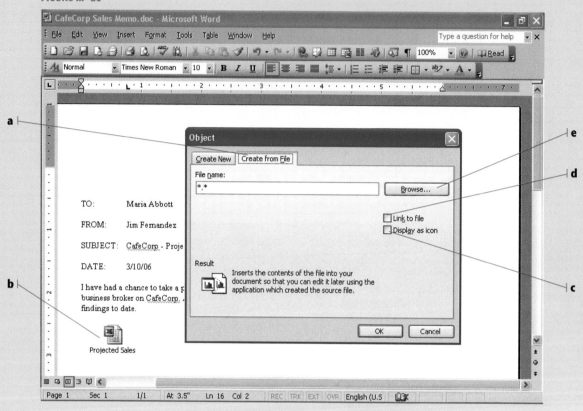

1. **Which element do you click to insert an existing object rather than creating a new file into a Word document?**
2. **Which element do you click to embed information that can be viewed by double-clicking an icon?**
3. **Which element do you double-click to display an embedded Excel worksheet?**
4. **Which element do you click to insert an object that maintains a connection to the source document?**
5. **Which element do you click to find a file to be embedded or linked?**

Match each term with the statement that best describes it.

6. **Destination document**
7. **Embedding**
8. **Source document**
9. **Linking**
10. **Table**
11. **Presentation graphics program**

a. File from which the object to be embedded or linked originates
b. Copies an object and retains a connection with the source program and source document
c. Document receiving the object to be embedded or linked
d. An Excel list converted to Access format
e. Copies an object and retains a connection with the source program
f. Used to create slide shows

Select the best answer from the list of choices.

12. An ASCII file:
    a. Contains text but no formatting
    b. Contains an unformatted worksheet
    c. Contains a PowerPoint presentation
    d. Contains formatting but no text

13. **An object consists of:**
    a. Text, a worksheet, or any other type of data
    b. Text only
    c. A worksheet only
    d. Database data only

14. **A purple triangle in the lower-right corner of a cell is a:**
    a. Field tag
    b. Table tag
    c. Smart tag
    d. Information tag

15. **To view a worksheet that has been embedded as an icon in a Word document, you need to:**
    a. Click View, then click Worksheet.
    b. Drag the icon.
    c. Double-click the worksheet icon.
    d. Click File, then click Open.

16. **A field that contains unique information for each record in a database table is called a:**
    a. Header key
    b. ID Key
    c. First key
    d. Primary key

▼ SKILLS REVIEW

1. **Import a text file.**
   a. Start Excel, open the tab-delimited text Data File titled EX M-9.txt from the drive and folder where your Data Files are stored, then save it as a Microsoft Office Excel workbook with the name **CafeCorp New Products**.
   b. Widen the columns as necessary so that all the data is visible.
   c. Format the data in columns B and C using the Accounting style with two decimal places.
   d. Center the column labels and apply bold formatting.
   e. Add your name to the left section of the worksheet footer, save the workbook, print the list in portrait orientation, then close the workbook.

2. **Import a database table.**
   a. In the Excel program, use the Import External Data command on the Data menu to import the Access Data File EX M-10.mdb from the drive and folder where your Data Files are stored, then save it as a Microsoft Office Excel workbook named **CafeCorp January Budget**.
   b. Rename the sheet **Budget**.
   c. Change the column labels so they read as follows: **Budget Category**, **Budget Item**, **Month**, and **Amount Budgeted**.
   d. Center the column labels and adjust the column widths as necessary.
   e. Use AutoSum to calculate a total in cell D26.
   f. Format range D2:D26 using the Accounting style with no decimal places.
   g. Save the workbook.

▼ SKILLS REVIEW (CONTINUED)

3. Insert a graphic file in a worksheet.

    a. Add four rows above row 1 to create space for a graphic.

    b. In rows 1 through 4, insert the picture file EX M-11.jpg from the drive and folder where your Data Files are stored.

    c. Resize and reposition the picture as necessary to make it fit in rows 1 through 4.

    d. Lower the contrast and the brightness of the picture.

    e. Remove the light blue background in the picture by making it transparent.

    f. Add your name to the left section of the worksheet footer, save the workbook, then print the worksheet.

4. Embed a worksheet.

    a. In cell A33, enter **For details on CafeCorp salaries, click this icon:**.

    b. In cell D33, use the Object dialog box to embed the worksheet object EX M-12.xls from the drive and folder where your Data Files are stored, displaying it as an icon with the caption **Salary Details**.

    c. Reposition the icon as necessary, double-click it to verify that the worksheet opens, then close it.

    d. Save the workbook, print the Budget worksheet, then close the workbook.

5. Link a worksheet to another program.

    a. Start Word, create a memo header addressed to your instructor, enter your name in the From line, enter **January Salaries** as the subject, and enter the current date in the Date line.

    b. In the memo body, link the spreadsheet object EX M-12.xls, displaying the worksheet, not an icon.

    c. Save the document as **January Salaries** in the drive and folder where your Data Files are stored, note that John Kelley's salary is $6,800. Close the document.

    d. Open the EX M-12 workbook in Excel and change John Kelley's salary to $7,000.

    e. Open the **January Salaries** document in Word, updating the links, and verify that John Kelley's salary has changed to $7,000 and that the new total salaries amount is $49,940.

    f. Save the **January Salaries** document, print the memo, then close the document and exit Word.

    g. Close the EX M-12 workbook without saving changes, then exit Excel.

6. Embed an Excel chart into a PowerPoint slide.

    a. Start PowerPoint.

    b. Open the PowerPoint Data File EX M-13.ppt from the drive and folder where your Data Files are stored, then save it as **Monthly Budget Meeting**.

    c. Display Slide 2, January Expenditures.

    d. Embed the Excel file EX M-14.xls from the drive and folder where your Data Files are located into Slide 2.

    e. View the slide in Slide Show view.

    f. Press [Esc] to return to Normal view.

    g. Replace the name Anna Smith with your name on the first slide.

    h. Save the presentation, print slides one and two as a handout (two slides to a page), then exit PowerPoint. (*Hint*: In the Print dialog box change Slides in the Print what section to Handouts, then select 2 in the slides per page section under Handouts.)

7. Import a list into an Access table.

    a. Start Access.

    b. Create a blank database named **Budget List** on the drive and folder where your Data Files are stored.

    c. Use the Get External Data option on the File menu to import the Excel list in the January Budget of EX M-15.xls from the drive and folder where your Data Files are stored. Use the first row as column headings, store the data in a new table, let Access add the primary key, and use the default table name January Budget.

    d. Open the January Budget table in Access and widen the columns as necessary to fully display the field names and field information.

    e. Enter your name in the Budget category column of row 25 in the table, save the database file, print the table, then exit Access.

▼ INDEPENDENT CHALLENGE 1

You are a loan officer for the Naples, Florida, branch of EastWest bank. You have been asked to give a presentation to a group of bank vice presidents about the types and number of loan applications your branch has received in the past year. To illustrate your loan data, you will add an Excel chart to one of your slides, showing the most popular loan types and the number of applications received this year for each type.

TABLE M-2

Loan type	Number of applications
Fixed home loans	1600
New car loans	7000
Used car loans	5400
Adjustable home loans	970
Boat loans	400

a. Start Excel, create a new workbook, then save it as **Consumer Loans** in the drive and folder where your Data Files are stored.

b. Enter the loans and the corresponding number of applications shown in Table M-2 into the Consumer Loans workbook. Name the sheet with the loan data **Loans**.

c. Create a 3-D pie chart from the loan data on a new sheet. Increase the font size to 20 in the legend. If a title appears on the chart, delete it. Your chart should look like Figure M-21.

d. Save the workbook with the chart sheet as the active sheet, then close the workbook.

e. Start PowerPoint, open the PowerPoint Data File EX M-16.ppt from the drive and folder where your Data Files are stored, then save it as **Loan Presentation**.

f. Embed the Excel chart from the Consumer Loans workbook into Slide 2.

g. View the slide in Slide Show view, then press [Esc] to end the show.

h. Edit Slide 1 to replace Allen Oles with your name, then save the presentation.

i. Print Slides 1 and 2 as a handout with two slides to a page, then close the presentation and exit PowerPoint.

FIGURE M-21

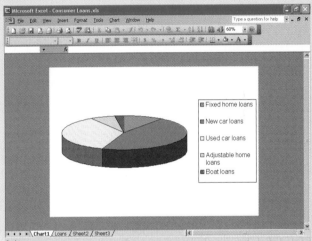

▼ INDEPENDENT CHALLENGE 2

You are opening a new store, Bridge Blades, that rents in-line skates in San Francisco, California. The owner of Gateway In-line, a similar store in San Francisco, is retiring and has agreed to sell you a text file containing his list of supplier information. You need to import this text file into Excel so that you can manipulate the data. Later you will convert the Excel file to an Access table, so that you can give it to your partner who is building a supplier database.

a. Start Excel, open the Data File titled EX M-17.txt from the drive and folder where your Data Files are stored, then save it as an Excel file named **Skate Supplier List**. (*Hint*: This is a tab-delimited text file.)

b. Adjust the column widths as necessary. Rename the worksheet **Supplier List**.

c. Center the column labels and apply bold formatting.

d. Sort the worksheet data in ascending order, first by Item, then by Supplier. (*Hint*: Open the Sort dialog box by clicking Sort on the Data menu, select Item in the first Sort by text box and Supplier in the second Then by text box.) Your worksheet should look like Figure M-22.

FIGURE M-22

	Supplier	Address	City	State	Zip	Phone	Contact	Item
1	Supplier	Address	City	State	Zip	Phone	Contact	Item
2	Cool Threads	232 Corn Ave	Daly City	CA	94623	415-465-7855	O. Rolins	Active wear
3	Head Start	102 Lake Dr	San Diego	CA	93112	212-223-9934	S. Werthen	Helmets
4	West Coast Helmets	8 High St	San Jose	CA	94671	408-332-9981	K. McGuire	Helmets
5	Jones Skates	394 19th Ave	San Francisco	CA	94554	415-444-9932	L. Smith	In-line skates
6	Rolling Around	343 Upham St	Los Angeles	CA	93111	213-887-4456	P. Newhal	In-line skates
7	SkateOn	12 Jean St	Oakland	CA	94611	510-422-9923	R. Jurez	In-line skates
8	Little Skate Mate	223 Main St	Ventura	CA	93143	213-332-5568	A. Blume	Misc parts
9	Uphill Skates	PO Box 9870	Milpitas	CA	94698	408-345-9343	F. Gerry	Misc parts
10	Gloves Unlimited	77 Sunrise St	Malibu	CA	93102	213-223-5432	J. Walsh	Protective gloves
11	Skate Pro	998 Little St	San Francisco	CA	94622	415-665-7342	W. Kitter	Protective gloves
12	Happy Skate	44 West St	Brisbane	CA	94453	415-223-9912	H. Jones	Safety pads
13	Pad Plus	33 Jackson St	Fresno	CA	96899	608-332-8790	J. Jerry	Safety pads
14								

Excel 2003

▼ INDEPENDENT CHALLENGE 2 (CONTINUED)

e. Add your name to the left section of the worksheet footer, print the worksheet in landscape orientation, save and close the workbook, then exit Excel.

f. Start Access, create a new blank database on the drive and folder where your Data Files are stored. Name the new database **Supplier List**.

g. Use the Get External Data option on the File menu to import the Excel file **Skate Supplier List** from the drive and folder where your Data Files are stored. Use the column labels as the field names, store the data in a new table, let Access add the primary key, and accept the default table name.

h. Open the Supplier List table and AutoFit the columns.

i. Enter your name in the Supplier column in row 13, save and print the table in landscape orientation so it fits on one page (adjust column width as necessary), then close it and exit Access.

▼ INDEPENDENT CHALLENGE 3

You are the newly hired manager at ReadIt, an independent bookstore in your town. An employee, Joy Yee, has complained that she is underpaid and would like a raise. You have examined the salaries of the employees of the company and agree with Joy. You will present this information to the owner of the bookstore and request permission to grant Joy Yee an increase in salary.

a. Start Word, open the Word file EX M-18.doc from the drive and folder where your Data Files are stored, then save it as **Salary Adjustment**.

b. Add your name to the From line of the memo and change the date to the current date.

c. At the end of the memo, embed the worksheet object EX M-19.xls as an icon from the drive and folder where your Data Files are stored, then double-click the icon to verify that the worksheet opens.

d. Return to Word, delete the icon for EX M-19 and link the spreadsheet object EX M-19 to the memo, displaying the worksheet, not an icon.

e. Save the Salary Adjustment memo and close the file.

f. Open the EX M-19 workbook and change Joy Yee's salary to $7000.

g. Open the Salary Adjustment memo, updating the links, and make sure Joy Yee's salary is updated.

Advanced Challenge Exercise

- Delete the worksheet at the bottom of the Salary Adjustment memo. Copy the range A1:C10 from Sheet1 of the EX M-19 workbook to the Clipboard.
- Return to the Salary Adjustment memo and use the Paste Special dialog box to paste a link to the range A1:C10 from EX M-19 that is on the Clipboard. Use Figure M-23 as a guide.
- Change Joy Yee's salary to $8000 in EX M-19. Update the links to display the new salary information in the Salary Adjustment memo.

FIGURE M-23

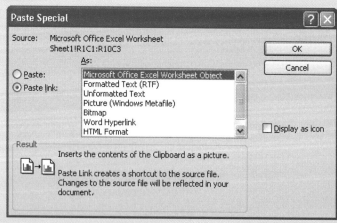

h. Save and print the memo.

i. Close the memo and exit Word.

j. Close EX M-19 without saving the change to Joy Yee's salary, then exit Excel.

▼ INDEPENDENT CHALLENGE 4

You are an assistant to the vice president of Sunshine Temporary, a temporary agency located in Winnipeg, Manitoba. Presently, Sunshine Temporary contracts with local companies to staff temporary secretarial and data entry positions. Management is considering adding permanent and temporary technical positions to the job titles it currently helps its clients fill. The vice president has asked you to prepare an Excel workbook showing the current open positions in the Sunshine Temporary database; she also wants you to include information about professional positions for which companies in the United States and Canada are recruiting. You will import a database list of current openings at Sunshine Temporary into an Excel workbook. Then you will use the Web to research professional positions in the United States and Canada and enter that information in the workbook.

a. Start Excel, import the Access file titled EX M-20.mdb from the drive and folder where your Data Files are stored, then save it as an Excel workbook titled **Temp Jobs**.

b. Rename the sheet tab **Open Positions**.

c. Format the data in column C using the Accounting style with two decimal places.

d. Sort the worksheet data in ascending order by Position.

e. Enter **Average Hourly Rate** in cell B14, then use the AutoSum list to enter a function in cell C14 that averages the Hourly Rates in column C.

f. Add four rows above row 1 to create space for a picture, and insert the file EX M-21.bmp from the drive and folder where your Data Files are stored. Resize the graphic as necessary to fit in rows 1 through 4.

g. Apply the List 1 AutoFormat to the range A5:C16. Compare your worksheet to Figure M-24.

h. Open your Web browser and go to the search engine of your choice. Search for job postings for six technical positions in the United States and Canada. Note the following information from the job postings: job title, city, state or province, and country.

i. Rename Sheet2 **Technical Positions**. On the Technical Positions sheet, enter the label **Position** in cell A1, **City** in cell B1, **State/Province** in cell C1, and **Country** in cell D1. Resize the columns as necessary. Use the information from your Web search to enter six records on the sheet.

j. Apply the List 3 AutoFormat to the range A1:D7.

FIGURE M-24

Excel 2003

Advanced Challenge Exercise

- Add four rows above row 1 in the Technical Positions worksheet and insert the picture EX M-21.bmp.
- Resize the picture as necessary to fit in rows 1 through 4.
- Crop the right side of the picture to remove the text. Crop the picture to remove the borders.
- Rotate the picture ten degrees.

k. Enter your name in the left section of both sheet footers, save the workbook, then print both worksheets.

l. Close the workbook, then exit Excel.

▼ VISUAL WORKSHOP

Create the worksheet shown in Figure M-25. Insert the graphic file EX M-22.jpg and embed the workbook file EX M-23.xls as an icon with the caption shown. Both files are located in your Data Files folder. Resize both objects as necessary. Enter your name in the left section of the worksheet footer, save the workbook as **Atlantic Price List**, then print the worksheet and exit Excel.

FIGURE M-25

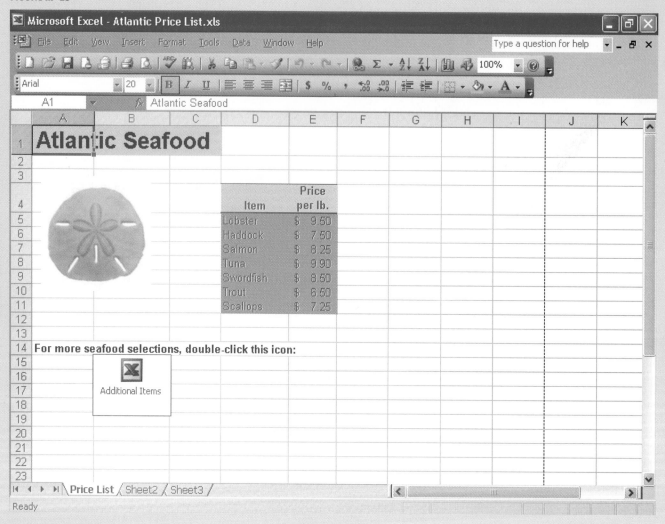

Customizing Excel and Advanced Worksheet Management

OBJECTIVES

Find files
Audit a worksheet
Outline a worksheet
Control worksheet calculations
Create custom AutoFill lists
Customize Excel
Add a comment to a cell
Create a template

If you have a SAM user profile, you may have access to hands-on instruction, practice, and assessment of the skills covered in this unit. Log in to your SAM account and go to your assignments page to see what your instructor has assigned.

Excel includes numerous tools and options designed to help you work as efficiently as possible. In this unit, you will learn how to use some of these elements to find errors and hide unnecessary detail. You'll also find out how to eliminate repetitive typing chores, save calculation time when using a large worksheet, and customize basic Excel features. Finally, you'll learn how to document your workbook and save it in a format that makes it easy to reuse. MediaLoft's assistant controller, Lisa Wong, routinely asks Jim Fernandez, MediaLoft's marketing manager, to help with a variety of spreadsheet-related tasks. You will use the numerous tools and options available in Excel to help Jim perform his work quickly and efficiently.

Finding Files

The Search task pane in Excel contains powerful searching tools that make it easy for you to find files. You can search for a file in several ways, such as by name or according to specific text located within a particular file. When searching for a file, you must specify one or more **criteria**, or conditions that must be met, to find your file. For example, you can specify that Excel should find only files that have the word "Inventory" in the filename and/or that were created after a particular date. ▬▬▬▬ Recently, Jim created a workbook that tracks the number of overtime hours employees worked in each MediaLoft store. He can't remember the exact name of the file, so he asks you to search for it by the first few letters of the filename.

STEPS

1. **Start Excel, click** File **on the menu bar, then click** File Search

   The Basic File Search task pane offers both basic and advanced search features. You can switch between the Basic and Advanced panes by using the first link at the bottom of the pane.

QUICK TIP

You can also search for text within Excel files. For example, if you know that your worksheet contains the text "Overtime hours," you can specify this in the "Search text:" text box of the Basic File Search task pane.

2. **In the Search pane, if Basic File Search appears in the title bar, click the** Advanced File Search **link; click** Remove All **to remove previous search criteria**

   All previous search conditions are cleared. You think the filename Jim needs starts with the prefix EX O but you're not sure of the remaining filename characters.

3. **Click the** Property list arrow, **click** File name, **make sure the Condition text box displays** includes, **click in the Value text box, then type** EX O*

   Be sure you type the letter "O" and not a zero. You use the **wildcard symbol** (*), or asterisk, to substitute for the remaining unknown characters. You need to specify where you want Excel to search for the file.

4. **Under Other Search Options, click the** Search in list arrow, **click the** Everywhere **check box to clear it if necessary, use the ⊞ sign to navigate to and select the check box next to the drive and folder that contains your Data Files, then click any cell in the worksheet**

5. **Click the** Results should be list arrow, **select** Excel Files **if it's not already selected, deselect any other files types, then click any cell in the worksheet**

   Compare your Advanced File Search task pane to Figure O-1.

QUICK TIP

If the search doesn't locate your file, click Modify, then try changing the Search in location to My Computer.

6. **Click** Go, **then click** Yes **to add the "File name" property to the search criteria**

   Five files are displayed that begin with "EX O". See Figure O-2. Once you have found the file you want, you can open and edit the file, create a new document based on the file, copy a link to the file to the Office Clipboard, or view the file's properties.

7. **Move the pointer over the** EX O-1.xls filename, **then click its** list arrow

   The options for file EX O-1 are listed, including an option to open the Properties dialog box.

8. **Click any cell in the worksheet, then click the file EX O-1.xls in the Search pane**

   The EX O-1 workbook opens.

9. **Close the Search Results pane, then save the workbook as** Overtime Hours **in the drive and folder where your Data Files are stored**

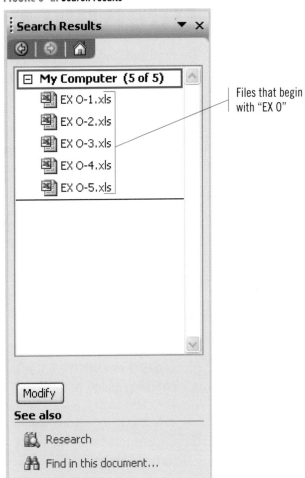

Files that begin with "EX O"

Clicking this dislays lower part of task pane

Link to Basic File Search

Clues to Use

Using file properties

Excel automatically tracks specific file properties, such as author name, file size, and file type, and displays them when you display file properties. To display a file's properties, right-click its name in the Search Results task pane or the Open dialog box and click Properties. In the [Filename] Properties dialog box, click the General tab to view general file information, the Custom tab to enter customized properties, and the Summary tab to enter a descriptive title, a subject, or keywords you can use in future searches. See Figure O-3. To search for a file by a specific property, in the Advanced File Search pane, select Text or property in the Property list, then enter the property text in the Value box.

FIGURE O-3: EX O-1 Properties dialog box

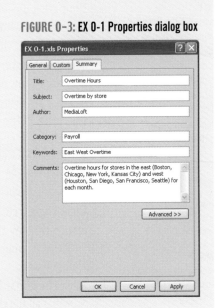

Excel 2003

Auditing a Worksheet

The Excel **auditing** feature helps you track errors and check worksheet logic. The Formula Auditing toolbar contains many error-checking tools to help audit a worksheet. Because errors can occur at any stage of worksheet development, it is important to include auditing as part of your workbook-building process. Jim asks you to help audit the worksheet that tracks the number of overtime hours at each store to verify the accuracy of the year-end totals. He also asks you to check for invalid overtime hours, which has been previously defined in the Data Validation dialog box to be any store's monthly amount that exceeds 60 hours. You will use the buttons on the Formula Auditing toolbar to identify errors in your worksheet.

STEPS

1. **Click** View **on the menu bar, point to** Toolbars, **click** Formula Auditing, **then click the** Error Checking button 🔷 **on the Formula Auditing toolbar**
   The Error Checking dialog box alerts you to an error in cell S6. The formula reads =R6/$R$16, indicating that the value in cell R6 will be divided by the value in cell R16. In Excel formulas, blank cells have a value of zero. That means the value in cell R6 cannot be divided by the value in cell R16 (zero) because division by zero is not mathematically possible. To correct the error, you must edit the formula so that it references cell R15, the grand total of overtime hours, not R16.

2. **Click** Edit in Formula Bar **in the Error Checking dialog box, edit the formula to read** =R6/$R$15, **click the** Enter button ✅ **on the formula bar, then click** Resume **In the Error checking dialog box**
   The edited formula produces the correct result, 9%, in cell S6. The Error Checking dialog box indicates an error from an inconsistent formula. Since this formula is correct you will ignore the warning.

3. **Click** Ignore Error, **then click** Ignore Error **three more times to ignore other inconsistent formula errors.**
   The Error Checking dialog box finds another division by zero error in cell S14. You decide to use another tool on the formula auditing toolbar to get more information about this error.

4. **Close the Error Checking dialog box, then click the** Trace Error button ⬇ **on the Formula Auditing toolbar**
   Tracer arrows, or **tracers**, point from cells that might have caused the error to the active cell containing the error, as shown in Figure O-4. The tracers extend from cells R14 and R16 to cell S14. To correct the error, you must edit the formula so that it references cell R15, the grand total of overtime hours, not R16.

QUICK TIP
To find cells to which a formula refers, click the cell containing the formula, then click the Trace Dependents button 🔷 on the Formula Auditing toolbar. To remove the Dependent tracer arrows, click the Remove Dependent Arrows button 🔷.

5. **Edit the formula in the formula bar to read** =R14/$R$15, **then click** ✅ **on the formula bar**
   Notice that the total for the Boston store in cell R5 is unusually high compared with the totals of the other stores. You can investigate this value by tracing the cell's **precedents**—the cells on which cell R5 depends.

6. **Click cell** R5, **click the** Trace Precedents button 🔷 **on the Formula Auditing toolbar, then scroll left until you see the tracer's starting point**
   The tracer arrow runs between cells B5 and R5, indicating that the formula in cell R5 reflects the quarterly *and* monthly totals of overtime hours. Only the quarterly totals should be reflected in cell R5.

7. **Click the** Remove Precedent Arrows button 🔷 **on the Formula Auditing toolbar, with cell R5 selected, click the** AutoSum button Σ **on the Standard toolbar, then press [Enter]**
   The tracer arrow disappears, the formula changes to sum only the quarterly totals, and the correct result, 524, appears in cell R5. Correcting the formula in cell R5 also adjusts the Grand Total percentage in cell S5 to 12%. You decide to check for invalid overtime hours that may have been entered in the worksheet.

QUICK TIP
To add validation criteria to selected worksheet cells, click Data, click Validation, then enter your validation criteria on the Settings tab of the Data Validation dialog box.

8. **Click the** Circle Invalid Data button 🔲 **on the Formula Auditing toolbar, then scroll to the left to display the May hours**
   The cells containing overtime hours exceeding 60 (the criterion previously defined for invalid data) are circled. See Figure O-5.

9. **Click the** Clear Validation Circles button 🔷, **return to cell A1, then save the workbook**
   Now that all the errors have been identified and corrected, you are finished auditing the worksheet.

FIGURE 0-4: Worksheet with traced error

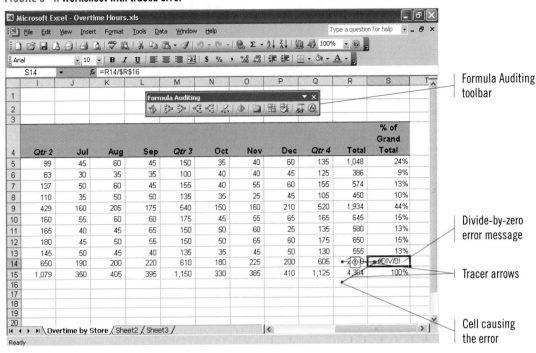

Formula Auditing toolbar

Divide-by-zero error message

Tracer arrows

Cell causing the error

FIGURE 0-5: Worksheet with invalid data circled

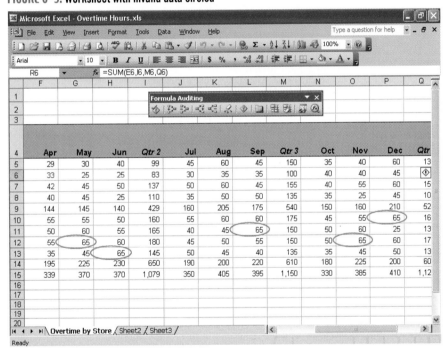

Clues to Use

Watching and evaluating formulas

As you edit your worksheet, you can watch the effect cell changes have on worksheet formulas. Select the cell or cells that you want to watch, click the Show Watch Window button 🔲 on the Formula Auditing toolbar, click Add Watch, then click Add. The Watch Window appears with the workbook name, worksheet name, the cell address you want to watch, the current cell value and its formula. As cell values that "feed into" the formula change, the resulting formula value in the Watch Window changes. You can also step through the evaluation of a formula, selecting the cell that contains a formula and clicking the Evaluate Formula button 🔲 on the Formula Auditing toolbar. The formula appears in the Evaluation Window and as you click the Evaluate button, the cell references are replaced with their values and the formula result is calculated.

Outlining a Worksheet

The Excel Outline command displays symbols that let you show only the critical rows and columns, such as subtotals or totals. To ensure that outlining displays useful results, it is important to structure your worksheet consistently: make sure that worksheet formulas "point" consistently in the same direction: Summary rows, such as subtotal rows, must be located below related data, and summary columns, such as grand total columns, must be located to the right of related data. (If you're not sure which way your formulas point, click the Trace Precedents button on the Formula Auditing toolbar.) You can outline an entire worksheet or a range of cells in a worksheet. ▓▓▓▓▓ Jim needs to give Lisa Wong, the MediaLoft assistant controller, the first and second quarter totals. He asks you to outline the first and second quarter information on the worksheet and to emphasize the subtotals for the East and West regions.

STEPS

QUICK TIP
You can group or ungroup a range of cells if the Auto Outline feature doesn't organize the worksheet data the way you want. Select the rows or columns you want to group, click Data on the menu bar, point to Group and Outline, then click Group or Ungroup.

1. **Select the cell range A1:I15, click Data on the menu bar, point to Group and Outline, then click Auto Outline**

   The first and second quarter information is displayed in Outline view, as shown in Figure O-6. There are several ways to change the amount of detail in an outlined worksheet, but the easiest is to use the column and row **outline symbols** in the upper-left corner of the worksheet, which hide varying levels of detail. The Row Level 1 symbol hides everything in the worksheet except the most important row or rows—in this case, the Grand Total row.

2. **Click the Row Level 1 button [1]**

   Only the heading and grand total appear. This selection doesn't display enough information, so you try the Row Level 2 button, which hides everything except the second most important rows—in this case, the subtotal rows and the Grand Total row.

3. **Click the Row Level 2 button [2]**

   Now you can see the rows you want. Next, you decide to display only the Qtr 1 and Qtr 2 columns.

QUICK TIP
If your summary information appears above your detail rows or to the left of your detail columns, you need to change the outline settings. Click Data on the menu bar, point to Group and Outline, then click Settings. The Settings dialog box will let you change the outline criteria.

4. **Click the Column Level 1 button [1]**

   The first and second quarter totals appear, and the monthly figures are no longer visible. You need a printed copy of the totals.

5. **Place your name in the left section of the worksheet footer, click File, click Print, click the Selection option button in the Print what area of the Print dialog box, then click Preview**

   The preview should look like Figure O-7.

6. **Click Print, click the Row Level 3 button [3], then click the Column Level 2 button [2]**

   The first and second quarterly monthly figures for each store reappear. You are finished using the outlining feature.

7. **Click Data on the menu bar, point to Group and Outline, then click Clear Outline**

   The Outline view closes, and the column and row level symbols are no longer visible. The worksheet returns to Normal view.

FIGURE O-6: Range in Outline view

Column outline symbols

Row outline symbols

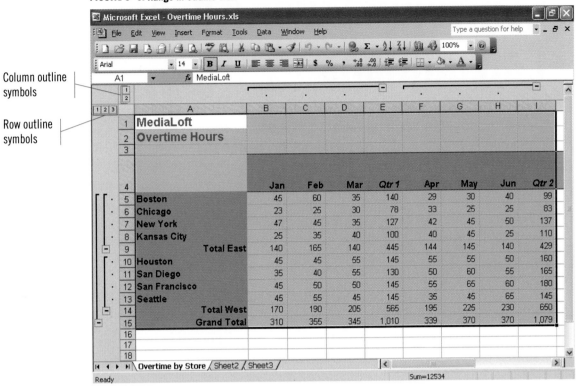

FIGURE O-7: Preview of outlined range

Subtotal rows

Total row

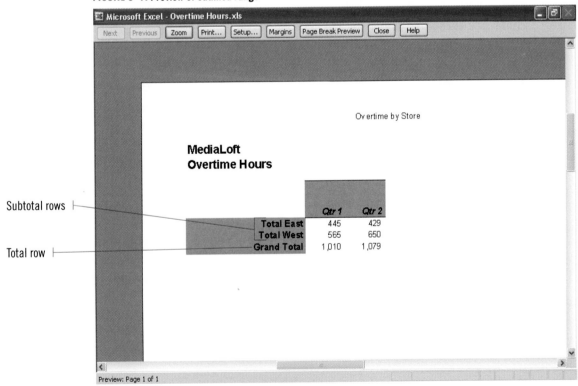

Controlling Worksheet Calculations

Whenever you change a value in a cell, Excel automatically recalculates all the formulas in the worksheet based on that cell. This automatic calculation is efficient until you create a worksheet so large that the recalculation process slows down data entry and screen updating. Worksheets with many formulas, data tables, or functions may also recalculate slowly. In these cases, you might want to selectively determine if and when you want Excel to perform calculations automatically. You do this by applying the **manual calculation** option. Once you change the calculation mode to manual, Excel applies manual calculation to all open worksheets. Because Jim knows that using specific Excel calculation options can help make worksheet building more efficient, he asks you to change from automatic to manual calculation.

STEPS

1. **Click Tools on the menu bar, click Options, then click the Calculation tab**

   The Calculation tab of the Options dialog box opens, as shown in Figure O-8.

QUICK TIP

To automatically recalculate all worksheet formulas except one- and two-input data tables, under Calculation, click Automatic except tables.

2. **Under Calculation, click to select the Manual option button**

   When you select the Manual option, the Recalculate before save box automatically becomes active and contains a check mark. Because the workbook does not recalculate until you save or close and reopen the workbook, you must make sure to recalculate your worksheet before you print it and after you make changes.

3. **Click OK**

   Jim informs you that the December total for the San Francisco store is incorrect. You decide to freeze the worksheet panes and adjust the entry in cell P12 accordingly.

4. **Click cell B5, click Window on the menu bar, click Freeze Panes, then scroll right to bring columns P through S into view**

   Notice that, in cell S12, San Francisco's percentage of the Grand Total is 15%.

5. **Click cell P12, type 10, then click the Enter button ☑ on the formula bar**

   The total formulas are *not* updated, and the percentage in cell S12 is still 15%. The word "Calculate" appears in the status bar to indicate that a specific value in the worksheet did indeed change and that the worksheet must be recalculated. See Figure O-9. You can press [F9] at any time to calculate all the open worksheets manually or [Shift][F9] to calculate just the active worksheet.

QUICK TIP

If a worksheet formula is linked to a worksheet that you have not recalculated and you update that link, you will see a message informing you of the situation. To update the link using the current value, click OK. To use the previous value, click Cancel.

6. **Press [Shift][F9], then save the workbook**

   The percentage in cell S12 is now 14% instead of 15%. The other formulas in the worksheet affected by the value in cell P12 changed as well. See Figure O-10. Because this is a relatively small worksheet that recalculates quickly, you will return to automatic calculation.

7. **Click Tools on the menu bar, click Options, click the Calculation tab if necessary, under Calculation click the Automatic option button, then click OK**

   Now any additional changes you make will automatically recalculate the worksheet formulas.

FIGURE O-8: Calculation tab of the Options dialog box

Calculation tab ⊢

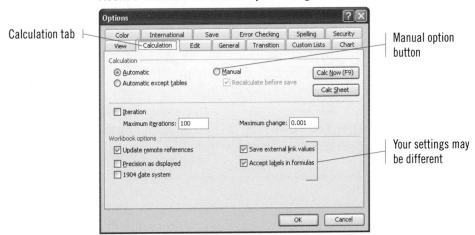

Manual option
button

Your settings may
be different

FIGURE O-9: Worksheet in manual calculation mode

Changed value ⊢

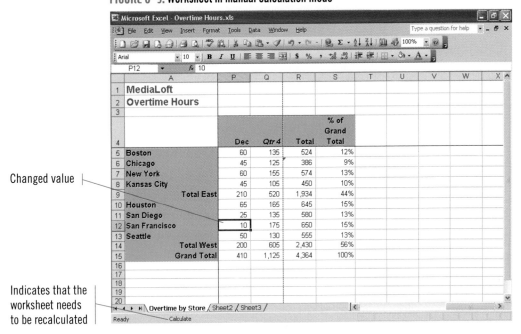

Indicates that the
worksheet needs
to be recalculated ⊢

FIGURE O-10: Worksheet with updated values

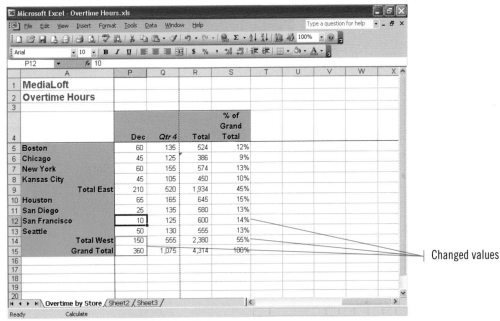

Changed values

Creating Custom AutoFill Lists

Whenever you need to type a list of words regularly, you can save time by creating a custom AutoFill list. Then you need only to enter the first value in a blank cell and drag the AutoFill handle. Excel will enter the rest of the information for you. Figure O-11 shows some examples of AutoFill lists built into Excel and of Custom AutoFill lists. ⬛⬛⬛⬛⬛ Jim often has to repeatedly enter MediaLoft store names and regional total labels in various worksheets. He asks you to create an AutoFill list to save time in performing this task. You begin by selecting the names and total labels in the worksheet.

STEPS

1. **Select the range** A5:A15

QUICK TIP

If a list of store locations already appears in the Custom lists box, the person using the computer before you forgot to delete it. Click the list, click Delete, then proceed with Step 3. It isn't possible to delete the four default lists for days and months.

2. **Click** Tools **on the menu bar, click** Options, **then click the** Custom Lists tab

   See Figure O-12. The Custom Lists tab shows the custom AutoFill lists that are already built into Excel. You want to define a custom list using the store information you selected in column A. The Import list from cells box contains the range you selected in Step 1.

3. **Click** Import

   The list of names is highlighted in the Custom lists box and appears in the List entries box. You will test the custom AutoFill list by placing it in a blank worksheet.

4. **Click** OK, **click the** Sheet2 tab, **type** Boston **in cell A1, then click the** Enter button ✓ **on the formula toolbar**

5. **Position the pointer over the AutoFill handle in the lower-right corner of cell A1**

   Notice that the pointer changes to ✛, as shown in Figure O-13.

QUICK TIP

You can also drag the AutoFill handle to the right to enter a custom list.

6. **Click and drag the pointer down to cell** A11, **then release the mouse button**

   The highlighted range now contains the custom list of store locations and total rows you created. You've finished creating and applying your custom AutoFill list, and you will delete it from the Options dialog box in case others will be using your computer.

7. **Click** Tools **on the menu bar, click** Options, **click the** Custom Lists tab **if necessary, click the list of store and region names in the Custom lists box, click** Delete, **click** OK **to confirm the deletion, then click** OK **again**

8. **Save and close the workbook**

FIGURE O-11: Sample AutoFill lists

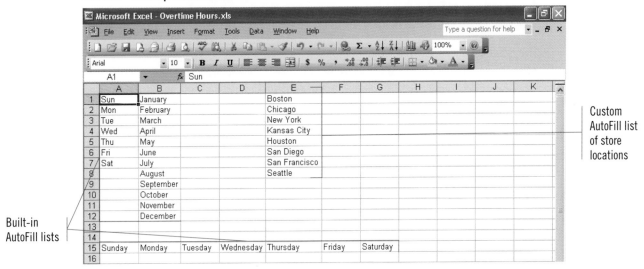

Custom AutoFill list of store locations

Built-in AutoFill lists

FIGURE O-12: Custom Lists tab

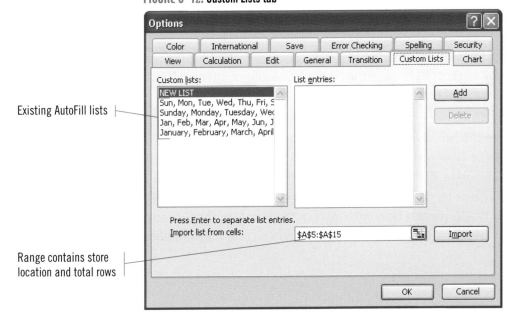

Existing AutoFill lists

Range contains store location and total rows

FIGURE O-13: Applying a custom AutoFill list

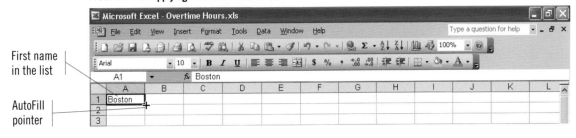

First name in the list

AutoFill pointer

Excel 2003

Customizing Excel

The Excel default settings for editing and viewing a worksheet are designed with user convenience in mind. You may find, however, that a particular setting doesn't always fit your needs, such as the default number of worksheets in a workbook. The thirteen tabs of the Options dialog box allow you to customize Excel to suit your work habits and needs. You've already used the Calculation tab to switch to manual calculation and the Custom Lists tab to create your own AutoFill list. The most commonly used Options dialog box tabs are explained in more detail in Table O-1.  Jim is curious about how he might customize Excel to allow him to work more efficiently. He asks you to use a blank workbook to explore some of the features of Excel available in the Options dialog box.

STEPS

1. **Click the New button** 🗋 **on the Standard toolbar, click Tools on the menu bar, click Options, then click the General tab**

   You would like to have five worksheets displayed rather than three when a new workbook is opened.

2. **Select 3 in the Sheets in new workbook text box, then enter 5**

   See Figure O-14. You can change the standard (default) font Excel displays in new workbooks.

3. **Click the Standard font list arrow, then select Book Antiqua**

   You can also change the standard workbook font size.

4. **Click the size list arrow, then select 12**

   These default settings take effect after you exit and restart Excel. Next, you'll check the default security settings.

5. **Click the Security tab, click Macro Security, click the Medium radio button if necessary, click OK, click OK to close the Options dialog box, then click OK to the message about quitting and restarting Excel**

   The Medium setting allows you to choose whether to enable macros when you open your workbooks.

6. **Close the workbook, exit Excel, then start Excel again**

   A new workbook opens with five sheet tabs and a 12-point Book Antiqua font. See Figure O-15. Now that you have finished exploring the Options dialog box, you need to reestablish the original Excel settings.

7. **Click Tools on the menu bar, click Options, click the General tab, select 5 in the Sheets in new workbook text box, enter 3, click the Standard font list arrow, select Arial, click the size list arrow, select 10, click OK twice, then close the workbook and exit Excel**

FIGURE O-14: General tab in the Options dialog box

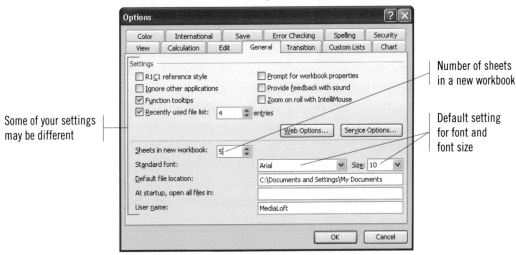

Some of your settings
may be different

Number of sheets
in a new workbook

Default setting
for font and
font size

FIGURE O-15: Workbook with new default settings

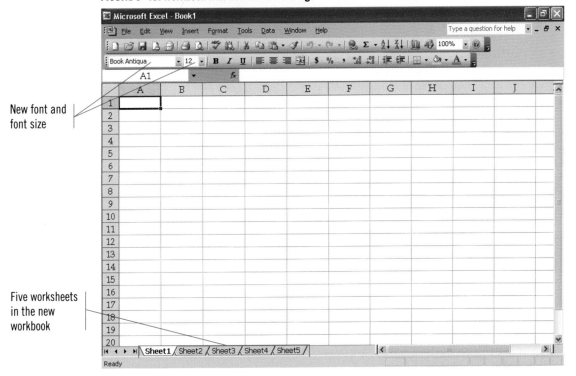

New font and
font size

Five worksheets
in the new
workbook

TABLE O-1: Selected Options dialog box tabs

tab	description
Calculation	Controls how the worksheet is calculated; choices include automatic and manual
Chart	Controls how empty cells are treated in a chart and whether chart tips are displayed
Color	Allows you to copy a customized color palette from one workbook to another
Custom Lists	Allows you to add or delete custom AutoFill lists
Edit	Controls the direction in which the cell selector moves after you press [Enter]; also contains other editing features
General	Controls the option to display the Properties dialog box when saving a workbook, the number of sheets in a new workbook, the default font in a workbook, and the drive and folder used in the Save dialog box by default; user name is also listed here
Transition	Provides options useful for users familiar with Lotus 1-2-3, and sets the default file type for saved worksheets
View	Controls the visibility of the formula bar, startup task pane, windows in taskbar, comments, status bar, gridlines, row and column headers, and scroll bars; also controls the option to display formulas in a worksheet

Adding a Comment to a Cell

If you plan to share a workbook with others, it's a good idea to **document**, or make notes about, basic assumptions, complex formulas, or questionable data. Reading your documentation, a coworker can quickly become familiar with your workbook. The easiest way to document a workbook is to use **cell comments**, which are notes attached to individual cells that appear when you place the pointer over a cell. When you sort or copy and paste cells, any comments attached to them will move to the new location. In PivotTable reports, however, the comments stay attached to the cell where they are entered. If the layout of the PivotTable changes, the comments do not move with the worksheet data. ▓▓▓▓▓ Jim thinks one of the figures in the worksheet may be incorrect. He asks you to add a comment for Lisa, pointing out the possible error. You will start by checking the default settings for comments in a workbook.

STEPS

1. **Start Excel, open Overtime Hours.xls from the drive and folder where your Data Files are stored, click Tools on the menu bar, click Options, click the View tab, click the Comment indicator only option button to select it if necessary, then click OK**
   The View tab allows you to display the comment and its indicator, the comment indicator only, or no comments. See Figure O-16.

2. **Right-click cell P12 on the Overtime by Store sheet, then click Insert Comment on the shortcut menu**
   The Comment box opens, as shown in Figure O-17. Excel automatically includes the computer's username at the beginning of the comment. The username is the name that appears on the General tab of the Options dialog box. Notice the white sizing handles on the border of the Comment box. You can drag these handles to change the size of the box.

   > **QUICK TIP**
   > You can also insert a comment by clicking the Comment option on the Insert menu or by clicking the New Comment button on the Reviewing or the Formula Auditing toolbar.

3. **Type Is this figure correct? It looks low to me.**
   The text automatically wraps to the next line as necessary.

4. **Click outside the Comment box**
   A red triangle appears in the upper-right corner of cell P12, indicating that a comment is attached to the cell. People who use your worksheet can easily display comments.

5. **Place the pointer over cell P12**
   The comment appears next to the cell. When you move the pointer outside of cell P12, the comment disappears. The worksheet is now finished and ready for printing.

6. **Click File on the menu bar, click Page Setup, click the Page tab if necessary, specify landscape orientation and fit the worksheet to one page**
   On a second printed page, you'll print only the cell comment along with its associated cell reference.

7. **Click the Sheet tab, under Print click the Comments list arrow, click At end of sheet, click Print, then click OK**
   Your comment is printed on a separate page after the worksheet.

8. **Save the workbook**

FIGURE O-16: View tab in the Options dialog box

Comment indicator
only button

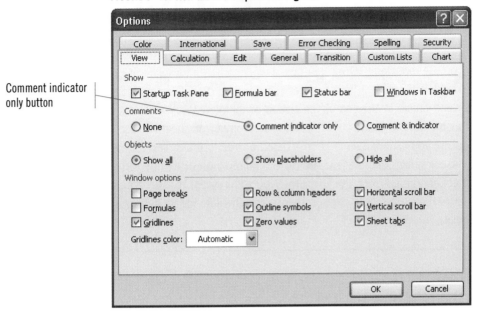

FIGURE O-17: Comment box

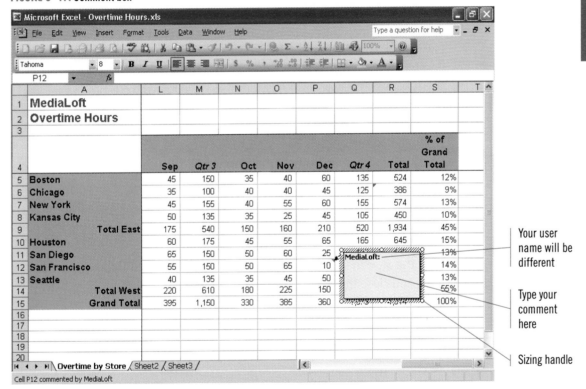

Your user
name will be
different

Type your
comment
here

Sizing handle

Clues to Use

Editing, copying, and deleting comments

To edit an existing comment, select the cell to which the comment is attached, click Insert on the menu bar, then click Edit Comment. You can also right-click a cell with a comment and click Edit Comment from the shortcut menu. To copy only comments, copy the cell contents, right-click the destination cell, select Paste Special, click Comments, then click OK. You can delete a comment by right-clicking the cell it is attached to, then selecting Delete Comment.

Creating a Template

A **template** is a workbook that contains text (such as column and row labels), formulas, macros, and formatting you use repeatedly. Once you save a workbook as a template, it provides a model for creating a new workbook without your having to reenter standard data. Excel provides access to templates on your computer and online in the Templates section of the New Workbook task pane. In most cases, though, you'll probably want to create your own template from a worksheet you use regularly. When you save a file as a template, you can create workbooks based on the formulas and formatting in the template and the template itself remains unchanged. ▰▰▰▰ Jim plans to use the same formulas, titles, frozen panes, and row and column labels from the Overtime Hours worksheet for subsequent yearly worksheets. He asks you to delete the extra sheets, the comments, and the data for each month, and then save the workbook as a template.

STEPS

1. **Click the** Sheet2 tab, **hold down** [Ctrl], **click the** Sheet3 tab, **right-click the** Sheet3 tab, **click** Delete, **then click** Delete **again**

2. **Right-click cell** P12, **then click** Delete Comment

    Now that you've removed the extra sheets and the comment, you'll delete the data on overtime hours. You'll leave the formulas in rows 9, 14, and 15, and in columns E, I, M, Q, R, and S, however, so that another user can simply begin entering data without having to re-create the formulas.

3. **Select the range** B5:D8, **press and hold** [Ctrl], **select the ranges** B10:D13, F5:H8, F10:H13, J5:L8, J10:L13, N5:P8, **and** N10:P13, **press** [Delete], **then click any cell in the worksheet to deselect the ranges**

    See Figure O-18. The hyphens in the subtotal and total rows and columns indicate that the current value of these cells is zero. The divide-by-zero error messages in column S are only temporary and will disappear as soon as you open the template, save it as a workbook, and begin to enter next year's data. To make the template easier to use, it's best to have the first data entry cell selected when you save it.

4. **Scroll left to bring columns B through G into view, then click cell** B5

5. **Click** File, **click** Save As, **click the** Save as type list arrow, **then click** Template

    Excel adds the .xlt extension to the filename and automatically switches to the Templates folder, as shown in Figure O-19. If you are using a computer on a network, you may not have permission to save to the Templates folder. You'll save your template to the drive and folder where your Data Files are stored instead.

6. **Click the** Save in list arrow, **click the drive and folder containing your Data Files, click** Save, **print and close the workbook, then exit Excel**

    Next year, when Jim needs to compile the information for overtime hours, he can simply open a document based on the Overtime Hours template (apply the template) and begin entering data.

Clues to Use

Applying and editing templates

To create a document based on a template (that is, to **apply** a template to a new document) you have saved in the Templates folder, open the New Workbook task pane, then under Templates, click On my computer. In the Templates dialog box, click the General tab, click the template you want to use, then click OK. Excel creates a new document named [Template Name]1. Save it as you would any new Excel document. The Spreadsheet Solutions tab lets you access several ready-made templates designed for business-related tasks.

The Templates section of the task pane also contains links to templates you might have previously stored on the Web and to templates on the Microsoft Office Web site. To edit a template, you must open the template itself (the .xlt file), change it, then save it under the same name. The changes are applied only to new documents you create; the changes do not affect documents you've already created using the template.

FIGURE O-18: Preparing the template

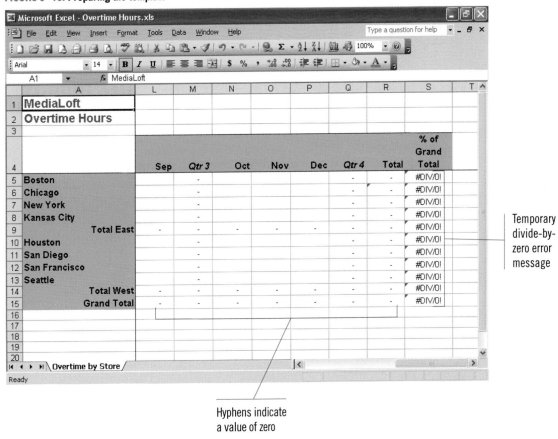

	L	M	N	O	P	Q	R	S	T
1 MediaLoft									
2 Overtime Hours									
3									
4	**Sep**	*Qtr 3*	**Oct**	**Nov**	**Dec**	*Qtr 4*	**Total**	**% of Grand Total**	
5 Boston		-				-	-	#DIV/0!	
6 Chicago		-				-	-	#DIV/0!	
7 New York		-				-	-	#DIV/0!	
8 Kansas City		-				-	-	#DIV/0!	
9 Total East	-	-	-	-	-	-	-	#DIV/0!	
10 Houston		-				-	-	#DIV/0!	
11 San Diego		-				-	-	#DIV/0!	
12 San Francisco		-				-	-	#DIV/0!	
13 Seattle		-				-	-	#DIV/0!	
14 Total West	-	-	-	-	-	-	-	#DIV/0!	
15 Grand Total	-	-	-	-	-	-	-	#DIV/0!	

Temporary divide-by-zero error message

Hyphens indicate a value of zero

FIGURE O-19: Saving a template

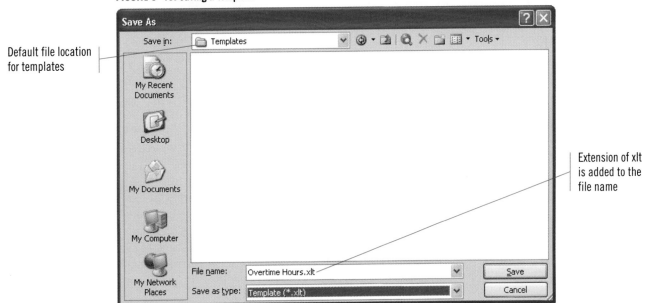

Default file location for templates

Extension of xlt is added to the file name

Save As
Save in: Templates

File name: Overtime Hours.xlt
Save as type: Template (*.xlt)

Practice

▼ CONCEPTS REVIEW

FIGURE O-20

Which element do you click to:

1. Evaluate a formula in a selected cell?
2. Trace the precedents of a selected cell?
3. Trace an error in a formula?

4. Watch the changes to a cell on a worksheet?
5. Circle invalid worksheet data?

Match each term with the statement that best describes it.

6. Note that appears when you place the pointer over a cell
7. Contains settings for customizing Excel
8. Calculates the worksheet manually

9. A workbook that contains text, formulas, and formatting
10. Automatically enters a list in a worksheet

a. Options dialog box
b. [Shift][F9]
c. Template
d. Comment
e. AutoFill

Select the best answer from the list of choices.

11. When searching for a file, which of these characters can substitute for unknown characters in a filename?
    a. #
    b. &
    c. *
    d. !
12. The _____ tab in the Options dialog box allows you to control the display of comments in a workbook.
    a. Properties
    b. Edit
    c. General
    d. View
13. The _____ automatically hides everything in the worksheet except the most important row or rows.
    a. Row Level 2 button
    b. Row Level 3 button
    c. Row Level 1 button
    d. Trace Error button
14. To apply a custom AutoFill list you:
    a. Press [Shift][F9].
    b. Click the AutoFill tab in the Edit dialog box.
    c. Select the list in the worksheet.
    d. Type the first cell entry and drag the AutoFill handle.

▼ SKILLS REVIEW

1. Find files.

a. Start Excel, open the Advanced Search pane.

b. Use the wildcard character (*) to enter the search criterion for all filenames that include EX O. Search in the drive and folder containing your Data Files. Limit the search to Excel files only. (*Hint:* Remember to clear previous search criteria.)

c. Display the properties for file EX O-2.xls.

d. Open the workbook EX O-2.xls from the Search Results task pane.

e. Close the Search Results task pane, then save the workbook as **Cafe Budget**.

2. Audit a worksheet.

a. Display the Formula Auditing toolbar and drag it to the bottom of the worksheet.

b. Select cell B10, then use the Trace Dependents button to locate all the cells that depend on this cell.

c. Clear the arrows from the worksheet using the Remove All Arrows button on the Formula Auditing toolbar.

d. Select cell B19, use the Trace Precedents button on the Formula Auditing toolbar to find the cells on which that figure is based, then correct the formula in cell B19. (*Hint:* It should be B7-B18.)

e. Use the Trace Error button on the Formula Auditing toolbar to trace the error in cell G6, then correct the formula. (*Hint:* It should be F6/F7.)

f. Use the Error Checking button on the Formula Auditing toolbar to check the worksheet for any other errors.

g. Use the Circle Invalid Data button on the Formula Auditing toolbar to locate any invalid data on the worksheet, then clear any validation circles.

h. Remove any arrows from the worksheet, close the Formula Auditing toolbar, then save the workbook.

3. Outline a worksheet.

a. Group the income information in rows 5 through 7. (*Hint:* Select rows 5 through 7, click Data on the menu bar, point to Group and Outline, then click Group.)

b. Hide the income information in rows 5 through 7 by clicking ⊟ to the lower left of row 7.

c. Enter your name in the worksheet header, then print the Budget worksheet with the income information hidden.

d. Redisplay the income rows by clicking ⊞.

e. Remove the row grouping. (*Hint:* With the grouped rows selected, click Data on the menu bar, point to Group and Outline, then click Ungroup.)

f. Click cell A1, then display the worksheet in Outline view.

g. Use the Row outline symbols to display only the Net Profit value in the budget.

h. Print the outlined worksheet.

i. Use the Row outline symbols to display all the rows in the budget.

j. Clear the outline from the worksheet.

4. Control worksheet calculations.

a. Open the Options dialog box.

b. Change the worksheet calculations to manual.

c. Change the figure in cell B6 to 33,000.

d. Recalculate the worksheet manually, using the appropriate key combination.

e. Turn off manual calculation and save the workbook.

5. Create custom AutoFill lists.

a. Select the range A4:A19.

b. Open the Custom Lists tab in the Options dialog box. Delete any custom lists except the four default day and month lists.

c. Import the selected text into the dialog box.

d. Close the dialog box.

e. On Sheet2, enter **Income** in cell A1.

f. With cell A1 selected, drag its fill handle to cell A15.

g. Select cell A1, and drag its fill handle to cell O1.

h. Enter your name in the Sheet2 footer, change the orientation to landscape, fit it to one page, then print it.

i. Open the Options dialog box again, delete the custom list you just created, then save the workbook.

▼ SKILLS REVIEW (CONTINUED)

6. Customize Excel.

    a. With Sheet2 still selected, open the Options dialog box.

    b. On the General tab, change the number of sheets in a new workbook to **4**.

    c. On the General tab, change the default font of a new workbook to 14-point Times New Roman.

    d. On the Security tab, set the macro security level to medium.

    e. Close the workbook and exit Excel.

    f. Start Excel and verify the new workbook's font is 14-point Times New Roman and that it has four worksheets.

    g. Reset the default number of worksheets to **3** and the default workbook font to 10-point Arial.

    h. Close the workbook and exit Excel.

7. Add a comment to a cell.

    a. Start Excel, open the Cafe Budget workbook from the drive and folder where your Data Files are stored. In the Budget sheet, select cell E12.

    b. Insert a comment in cell E12 using the shortcut menu.

    c. Type **Does this include TV and radio spots, or only newspaper and magazine advertising? It is very important to include these.**

    d. Drag the resize handles on the borders of the Comment box until you can see the entire comment.

    e. Click anywhere outside the Comment box to close it.

    f. Display the comment by moving the pointer over cell E12, then check it for errors.

    g. Edit the comment in cell E12 so it ends after the word **spots**, with a question mark at the end.

    h. Print the worksheet and your comment, with the comment appearing at the end of the sheet.

    i. Save the workbook.

8. Create a template.

    a. Delete Sheet2 and Sheet3.

    b. Delete the comment in cell E12.

    c. Delete the budget data for all four quarters. Leave the worksheet formulas intact.

    d. Select cell B5, then save the workbook as a template named **Budget Template**, in the folder where your Data Files are stored.

    e. Close the template, then open a document based on the template using the New Workbook task pane. (*Hint*: Use the From existing workbook option under New, click the Budget Template, then click Create New.)

    f. Enter your own data for all four quarters and in every budget category.

    g. Save the workbook as **Cafe Budget 2.xls** to the folder where your Data Files are stored.

    h. Print the Budget worksheet, then close the workbook and exit Excel.

▼ INDEPENDENT CHALLENGE 1

You are a manager at Life Skills, a nonprofit agency devoted to helping people with severe learning disabilities become proficient computer users. Your department specializes in hands-on instruction for software programs. During the month of October, you created a check register in Excel for department expenses. Before you begin generating a November register, however, you want to check the October register for errors. In your worksheet audit, you will look for miscalculated totals and formula errors. You will also add a comment to document the worksheet.

    a. Start Excel, open the Data File titled EX O-3.xls from the drive and folder where your Data Files are stored, then save it as **Check Register**.

    b. Select cell F16 and use the Trace Precedents button on the Formula Auditing toolbar to show the cells used in its formula.

    c. The balance in cell F16 does not reflect the hardware purchase on October 15th. Edit the formula to subtract the hardware expense from the previous balance. (*Hint*: The formula should be F15-E16.)

    d. Due to illness, your Excel instructor taught only two hours of a six-hour course. Create a comment indicating this in cell C19 to remind you that he owes you four hours.

    e. Use the Error Checking button to locate and fix any other errors in the worksheet. (*Hint*: Check cell E24.)

▼ INDEPENDENT CHALLENGE 1 (CONTINUED)

Advanced Challenge Exercise

- Evaluate the formula in cell F21 using the Evaluate Formula button on the Formula Auditing toolbar.
- In the Evalute Formula dialog box, click Evaluate three times to see the process of substituting values for cell addresses in the formula and the results of those formula calculations. Close the Evaluate Formula window.
- Open the Watch Window using the Show Watch Window button on the Formula Auditing toolbar. Click Add Watch to add cell E23 to the Watch Window and observe its value in the window as you change cell E6 to 1600. Close the Watch Window.

f. Add your name to the left section of the worksheet footer, preview the worksheet, then save the workbook. Use the Page Setup command on the File menu to print the worksheet and the comments. Close the workbook, then exit Excel.

▼ INDEPENDENT CHALLENGE 2

You are a manager at EarthSchool, a nonprofit agency located in Toronto, Ontario. Your agency's mission is to educate students in elementary school about environmental issues. One of your responsibilities is to keep track of your department's regular monthly expenses. Your assistant has compiled a list of fixed expenses in an Excel workbook but can't remember the filename. Once you find the file by using the search tools in the Search pane, you want to create a custom AutoFill list including each expense item to save time in preparing similar worksheets in the future. You will also temporarily switch to manual formula calculation, check the total formula, and document the data.

a. Start Excel, then use the Advanced File Search pane to find a file in the drive and folder where you Data Files are stored with the text **EarthSchool** in the workbook. (*Hint*: Choose **Text or property** in the Property text box, make sure the Condition text box displays **includes**, and enter **EarthSchool** in the Value text box. Make sure that you clear any previous search conditions.) Open the workbook.

b. Save the workbook as **Monthly Budget** in the drive and folder where your Data Files are stored, then close the Search Results task pane.

c. Select the range of cells **A6:A17** on the Fixed Expenses sheet, then open the Options dialog box and import the list into the Custom Lists tab.

d. Close the Options dialog box and use the AutoFill handle to insert your list in cells C1:C12 in Sheet2.

e. Add your name to the Sheet2 footer, save the workbook, then preview and print Sheet2.

f. Return to the Fixed Expenses sheet and delete your custom list from the Options dialog box.

g. Use the Options dialog box to switch to manual calculation.

h. Change the expense for Printer paper to 39.00. Calculate the worksheet formulas manually.

i. Turn on automatic calculation again.

j. Use the View tab on the Options dialog box to display comments and their indicators in a worksheet.

k. Add the comment **This may increase** to cell B6.

l. Trace the precedents of cell B18. Compare your worksheet to Figure O-21.

m. Remove the arrow from the worksheet, change the comments settings back to display comment indicators only.

FIGURE O-21

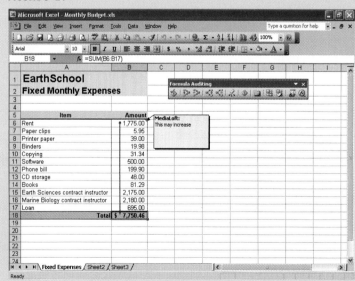

Advanced Challenge Exercise

- Edit the comment in cell B6 to **This may increase next month**.
- Paste the comment in cell B6 to cell B11.
- Delete the comment in cell B6.

▼ INDEPENDENT CHALLENGE 2 (CONTINUED)

n. Add your name to the left section of the worksheet footer, save the workbook, then print the Fixed Expenses worksheet with the comment appearing at the end of the sheet.

o. Close the workbook and exit Excel.

▼ INDEPENDENT CHALLENGE 3

Your business, Kidcare, helps parents find high-quality, in-home childcare. In exchange for a one-time fee, you recruit and interview potential nannies, confirm references, and conduct thorough background checks. In addition, once a nanny has been hired, you provide training in child development and infant first aid. Currently, you are preparing your budget for the next four quarters. After you enter the data for each expense and income category, you will create a condensed version of the worksheet using Excel outlining tools.

a. Start Excel, create a new workbook, then save it as **Kidcare** in the drive and folder where your Data Files are stored.

b. Using Figure O-22 as a guide, enter and format a title of **Yearly Budget**, then enter the following column labels: **Description, 1st Qtr, 2nd Qtr, 3rd Qtr, 4th Qtr**, and **Total**.

c. Enter labels for the following income items: **Nanny Fee, Child Development Course, CPR Course**, and **Income Total**. Enter labels for at least six office expense items and the Expenses Total. Create a row for net cash flow calculations. Format the worksheet appropriately.

d. Enter expenses and income data for each quarter. Total the income items and the expenses. Create formulas for the total column and the cash flow row (income minus expenses).

e. Check the outline settings to make sure the summary rows are below the detail rows and the summary columns are to the right of the detail columns. (*Hint*: Click Data, point to Group and Outline, then click Settings.)

f. Display the worksheet in Outline view.

g. Use the Row Level 1 button on the outline to display only the Net cash flow row, as shown in Figure O-22. Your net cash flow data and formatting will be different.

FIGURE O-22

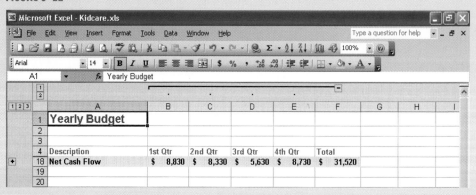

h. Add your name to the left section of the worksheet footer, save the workbook, then print the outlined worksheet.

i. Redisplay all the rows, then clear the outline.

j. Select the Yearly Budget title, the row labels, and the first and second quarter data and display them in Outline view.

k. Use the Row outline symbols to show only the Income Total, Expenses Total, and Net Cash Flow rows and their headings.

l. Preview the outlined first and second quarter information. Compare your preview to Figure O-23. Your data will be different.

m. Print the outlined first and second quarter information.

n. Clear the outline. Close the workbook and exit Excel.

FIGURE O-23

Yearly Budget		
Description	1st Qtr	2nd Qtr
Income Total	$ 11,200	$ 10,700
Expenses		
Expenses Total	$ 2,370	$ 2,370
Net Cash Flow	$ 8,830	$ 8,330

▼ INDEPENDENT CHALLENGE 4

As the marketing manager of products at NewSite, a Web development firm, you frequently travel to customer sites. After every trip, you submit an expense report for reimbursement of your travel expenditures. A template containing the input fields and formulas would speed up the process of preparing this report. You decide to research the templates available in the Microsoft Office template gallery to see if any are suitable for recording your travel expenses.

a. Start Excel, then use the link for Templates on Office Online in the New Workbook task pane to view the templates available on Microsoft Online. You must have an open Internet connection to connect to Microsoft Online and to download templates.

b. Search for an expense statement that might be suitable for recording your travel expenses. (*Hint*: Search on Expense statement.)

c. Download the template named Expense Report (with the Excel icon) in the list of links. (*Hint*: When you can see the template preview, you need to minimize your browser, close any open workbooks, exit from Excel, then maximize the browser window with the template preview and click Download Now. You need to exit Excel before downloading the template because Excel automatically starts during the download process.

d. Accept the licensing agreement and click continue on any dialog box if necessary. When the download is complete, Excel will start and the template will be displayed as a worksheet. Close the task pane.

e. Save the downloaded worksheet as a template to the folder containing your Data Files and name it **Expense Statement**.

FIGURE O-24

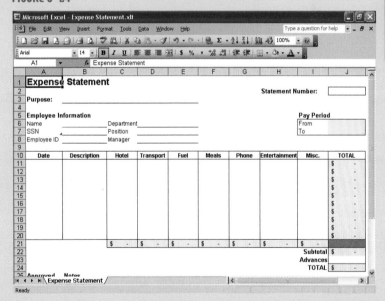

f. Edit the template to change the font color of the text in cell A2 to blue, delete row 1, and delete column B. Compare your edited template to Figure O-24.

g. Save the edited template then close the template.

h. Open a workbook based on the Expense Statement template. (*Hint*: Use the From existing workbook link on the New Workbook task pane.) Save the workbook as **My Expense Statement**.

i. Enter two lines of your own expense data for a business trip. Enter your name in the Name field. Widen columns as necessary.

j. Add **Includes all taxes** as a comment in cell C10.

k. Outline the worksheet and use the Row outline symbols to display only your employee information and the expense totals.

l. Print the outlined worksheet showing the total information. Clear the outline.

m. Save and close the workbook. Exit Excel and your browser.

▼ VISUAL WORKSHOP

Open the Data File EX O-5.xls from the drive and folder where your Data Files are stored, then save it as **Zoo Count**. Use the auditing and error correction techniques you have learned to correct any errors in the worksheet. Your calculated results should match Figure O-25. Make sure to include the comment in cell E21. Add your name to the left section of the worksheet footer, save the workbook, then preview and print the worksheet and comment. Close the workbook and exit Excel.

FIGURE O-25

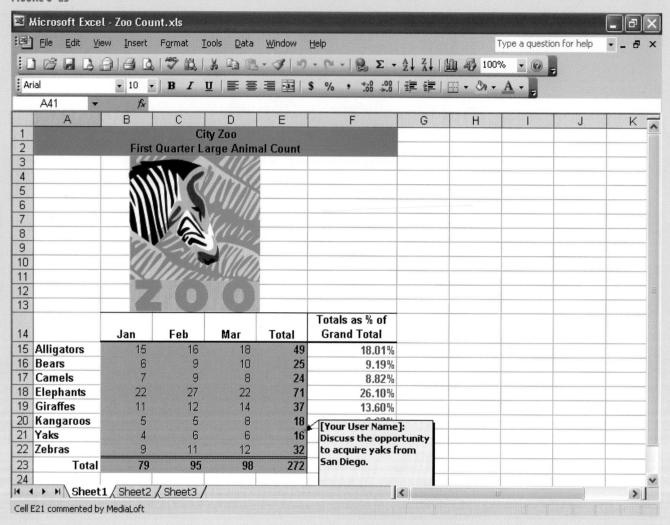

UNIT P
Excel 2003

Programming with Excel

OBJECTIVES

View VBA code
Analyze VBA code
Write VBA code
Add a conditional statement
Prompt the user for data
Debug a macro
Create a main procedure
Run a main procedure

If you have a SAM user profile, you may have access to hands-on instruction, practice, and assessment of the skills covered in this unit. Log in to your SAM account and go to your assignments page to see what your instructor has assigned.

All Excel macros are written in a programming language called Visual Basic for Applications, or simply, **VBA**. When you create a macro with the Excel macro recorder, the recorder writes the VBA instructions for you. You can also create an Excel macro by entering VBA instructions manually. The sequence of VBA statements contained in a macro is called a **procedure**. In this unit, you will view and analyze existing VBA code; then you will write VBA code on your own. You will learn how to add a conditional statement to a procedure, as well as how to prompt the user for information while the macro is running. You will also find out how to locate any errors, or bugs, in a macro. Finally, you will combine several macros into one main procedure. MediaLoft's marketing manager, Jim Fernandez, would like to automate some of the division's time-consuming tasks. You will help Jim by creating five Excel macros for the Marketing Department.

Viewing VBA Code

Before you can write Excel macro procedures, you must become familiar with the VBA (Visual Basic for Applications) programming language. A common method of learning any programming language is to view existing code. To view VBA code, you open the **Visual Basic Editor**, which contains a Project window, a Properties window, and a Code window. The VBA code for macro procedures appears in the Code window. The first line of a procedure, called the **procedure header**, defines the procedure's type, name, and arguments. Items that appear in blue are **keywords**, which are words Excel recognizes as part of the VBA programming language. **Comments**, which are notes explaining the code, appear in green, and the remaining code appears in black. You use the Visual Basic Editor to view or edit an existing macro as well as to create new ones. 🔳🔳🔳 Each week, MediaLoft receives a text file from the radio station KHOT, containing information about weekly radio ads. Jim has already imported the text file into a worksheet, but it still needs to be formatted. He asks you to work on a macro to automate the process of formatting this imported text file.

STEPS

TROUBLE

If you get a security error message when attempting to open your workbook, the security level may be set too high in the workbook. You can enable macros for the workbook by pointing to Macro on the Tools menu then clicking Security. Set the security level to Medium, then close and reopen the workbook.

1. **Start Excel, if necessary, open the Data File EX P-1.xls from the drive and folder where your Data Files are stored, click** Enable Macros, **then save it as** KHOT Procedures

   The security warning, shown in Figure P-1, alerts you that the worksheet contains macros. The KHOT Procedures workbook displays a blank worksheet. This is the workbook that you will use to create and store all the procedures for this lesson.

2. **Click** Tools **on the menu bar, point to** Macro, **then click** Macros

   The Macro dialog box opens with the FormatFile macro procedure in the list box. If you have any macros saved in your Personal Macro workbook they will also be listed in the Macro dialog box.

3. **If it is not already selected, click** FormatFile, **click** Edit, **then in the Project Explorer window shown in Figure P-2, under Modules click** Format **if it is not already selected**

   Because the FormatFile procedure is contained in the Format module, clicking Format selects the Format module and displays the FormatFile procedure in the Code window. See Figure P-2. See Table P-1 to make sure your screen matches those in the unit.

4. **Make sure both the Visual Basic window and the Code window are maximized to match Figure P-2**

5. **Examine the top three lines of code, which contain comments, and the first line of code beginning with Sub FormatFile( )**

   Notice that the different parts of the procedure appear in various colors. The first two comment lines give the procedure name and tell what the procedure does. The third line of comments explains that the keyboard shortcut for this macro procedure is [Ctrl][F]. The keyword Sub in the procedure header indicates that this is a **Sub procedure**, or a series of Visual Basic statements that perform an action but do not return a value. In the next lesson, you will analyze the procedure code to see what each line does.

TABLE P-1: Matching your screen to the unit figures

if...	do this...
The Properties or Project Explorer window is not displayed	Click the Properties Window button 📇 then click the Project Explorer button 📇 on the toolbar
You see only the Code window	Click Tools on the menu bar, click Options, click the Docking tab, then make sure the Project Explorer and Properties Window options are selected
You do not see folders in the Explorer window	Click the Toggle Folders button 📁 on the Project Explorer window Project toolbar

FIGURE P-1: Security warning dialog box

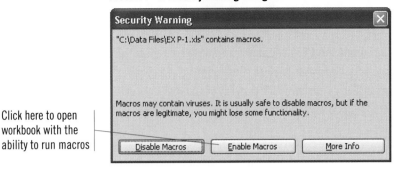

Click here to open
workbook with the
ability to run macros

FIGURE P-2: Procedure displayed in the Visual Basic Editor

Procedure
header

Project
Explorer
window

Properties
window

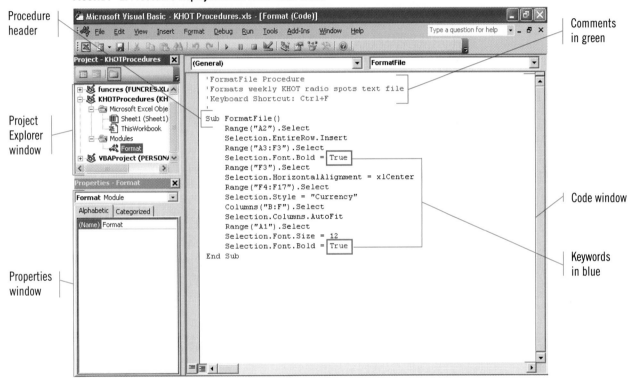

Comments
in green

Code window

Keywords
in blue

Clues to Use

Understanding the Visual Basic Editor

A **module** is the Visual Basic equivalent of a worksheet. In it, you store macro procedures, just as you store data in worksheets. Modules, in turn, are stored in workbooks (or projects), along with worksheets. A **project** is the collection of all procedures in a workbook. You view and edit modules in the Visual Basic Editor, which is made up of three windows, Project Explorer (also called the Project window), the Code window, and the Properties window. Project Explorer displays a list of all open projects (or workbooks) and the worksheets and modules they contain. To view the procedures stored in a module, you must first select the module in Project Explorer (just as you would select a file in Windows Explorer). The Code window then displays the selected module's procedures. The Properties window displays a list of characteristics (or properties) associated with the module. A newly inserted module has only one property, its name.

Analyzing VBA Code

You can learn a lot about the VBA language simply by analyzing the code generated by the Excel macro recorder. The more VBA code you analyze, the easier it is for you to write your own programming code. Before writing any new procedures, you will analyze a previously written one that applies formatting to a worksheet, then you will open a worksheet that you want to format and run the macro.

STEPS

1. **With the FormatFile procedure still displayed in the Code window, examine the next four lines of code, beginning with** `Range("A2").Select`

   See Figure P-3. Every element of Excel, including a range, is considered an **object**. A **range object** represents a cell or a range of cells. The statement Range("A2").Select selects the range object cell A2. Notice that several times in the procedure, a line of code (or **statement**) selects a range, and then subsequent lines act on that selection. The next statement, Selection.EntireRow.Insert, inserts a row above the selection, which is currently cell A2. The next two lines of code select range A3:F3 and apply bold formatting to that selection. In VBA terminology, bold formatting is a value of an object's Bold property. A **property** is an attribute of an object that defines one of the object's characteristics (such as size) or an aspect of its behavior (such as whether it is enabled). The properties of an object are listed in the Properties window. To change the characteristics of an object, you change the values of its properties. For example, to apply bold formatting to a selected range, you assign the value True to the range's Bold property. To remove bold formatting, assign the value False.

2. **Examine the remaining lines of code, beginning with** `Range ("F3").Select`

   The next two statements select the range object cell F3 and center its contents, then the following two statements select the F4:F17 range object and format it as currency. Column objects B through F are then selected and their widths set to AutoFit. Finally, the range object cell A1 is selected, its font size is changed to 12, and its Bold property is set to True. The last line, End Sub, indicates the end of the Sub procedure and is also referred to as the **procedure footer**.

3. **Click the View Microsoft Excel button ⊠ on the Visual Basic Editor Standard toolbar to return to Excel**

   Because the macro is stored in the KHOT Procedures workbook, Jim can open this workbook and use the macro stored there repeatedly each week after he receives that week's data. He wants you to open the workbook containing data for January 1–7 and run the macro to format that data. You must leave the KHOT Procedures workbook open to use the macro stored there.

4. **Open the workbook EX P-2.xls from the drive and folder where your Data Files are stored, then save it as KHOT Advertising**

   This is the workbook containing the data you want to format.

5. **Press [Ctrl][F] to run the procedure**

   The FormatFile procedure formats the text, as shown in Figure P-4.

6. **Save the workbook**

   Now that you've successfully viewed and analyzed VBA code and run the macro, you will learn how to write your own code.

FIGURE P-3: VBA code for the FormatFile procedure

Selects range object cell A2

Applies bold formatting to range A3:F3

Sets widths of columns B-F to AutoFit

Adjusts font size and bolds cell A1

Inserts a row above cell A2

Centers contents of cell F3

Formats range F4:F17 as currency

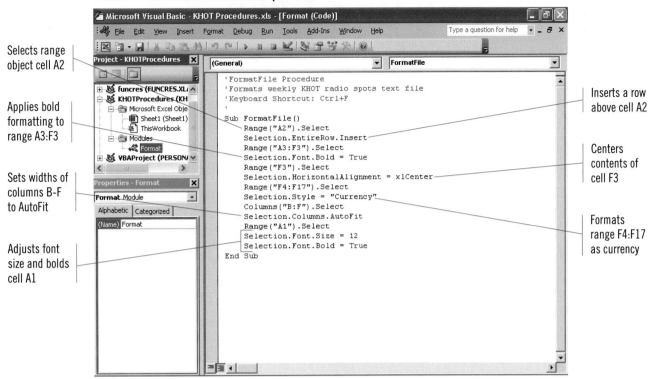

```
'FormatFile Procedure
'Formats weekly KHOT radio spots text file
'Keyboard Shortcut: Ctrl+F
'
Sub FormatFile()
    Range("A2").Select
    Selection.EntireRow.Insert
    Range("A3:F3").Select
    Selection.Font.Bold = True
    Range("F3").Select
    Selection.HorizontalAlignment = xlCenter
    Range("F4:F17").Select
    Selection.Style = "Currency"
    Columns("B:F").Select
    Selection.Columns.AutoFit
    Range("A1").Select
    Selection.Font.Size = 12
    Selection.Font.Bold = True
End Sub
```

FIGURE P-4: Worksheet formatted using the FormatFile procedure

Formatted title

Row inserted

Columns widened

Formatted column headings

Range formatted as currency

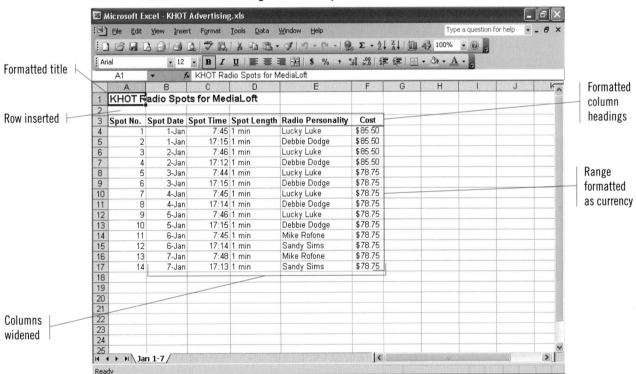

Writing VBA Code

To write your own code, you first need to open the Visual Basic Editor and add a module to the workbook. You can then begin entering the procedure code. In the first few lines of a procedure, you typically include comments indicating the name of the procedure, a brief description of the procedure, and shortcut keys, if applicable. When writing Visual Basic code for Excel, you must follow the formatting rules, or **syntax**, of the VBA programming language exactly. A misspelled keyword or variable name causes a procedure to fail. ▆▆▆▆ Jim would like to total the cost of the radio ads. You will help him by writing a procedure that automates this routine task.

STEPS

TROUBLE

If the Code window is empty, verify that the workbook that contains your procedures (KHOT Procedures) is open.

1. **With the Jan 1-7 worksheet still displayed, click** Tools **on the menu bar, point to** Macro, **then click** Visual Basic Editor

   Two projects are displayed in the Project Explorer window, KHOT Procedures (which contains the Format macro) and KHOT Advertising Jan 1-7 (which contains the weekly data). The FormatFile procedure is again displayed in the Visual Basic Editor. You may have other projects in the Project Explorer window.

2. **Click the** Modules folder **in the KHOT Procedures project**

   You will store all of the procedures in the KHOT Procedures project, which is in the KHOT Procedures workbook. By clicking the Modules folder, you have activated the workbook, as you can see in the title bar.

3. **Click** Insert **on the Visual Basic Editor menu bar, then click** Module

   A new, blank module, with the default name Module1, is inserted in the KHOT Procedures workbook. The property name of the module could be more descriptive.

QUICK TIP

As you type, you may see words in drop-down lists. This optional feature is explained in the Clues to Use titled "Entering code using the scrollable word list" on the next page. For now, just continue to type.

4. **Click** (Name) **in the Properties window, then type** Total

   The module name is Total. The module name should not be the same as the procedure name (which will be AddTotal). In the Figure P-5 code, comments begin with an apostrophe, and the lines of code under Sub AddTotal( ) have been indented using the Tab key. When you enter the code in the next step, after you type Sub AddTotal( ) (the procedure header) and press [Enter], the Visual Basic Editor automatically enters End Sub (the procedure footer) in the Code window.

5. **Click in the** Code window, **then type the procedure code exactly as shown in Figure P-5**

   The lines that begin with ActiveCell.Formula insert the information enclosed in quotation marks into the active cell. For example, ActiveCell.Formula = "Weekly Total:" inserts the words Weekly Total: into cell E18, the active cell. The With clause near the bottom of the procedure is used to repeat several operations on the same object. As you type each line, Excel adjusts the spacing. Press [Tab] to indent text and [Shift][Tab] to move the insertion point to the left.

6. **Compare the procedure code you entered in the Code window with Figure P-5; if necessary, make any corrections, then click the** Save KHOT Procedures.xls button 🔳 **on the Visual Basic Editor Standard toolbar**

7. **Click the** View Microsoft Excel button 🗷 **on the toolbar, if necessary, click** KHOT Advertising.xls **on the taskbar to display the worksheet; with the Jan 1-7 worksheet displayed, click** Tools **on the Excel menu bar, point to** Macro, **then click** Macros

   Macro names have two parts. The first part ('KHOT Procedures.xls'!) indicates the workbook where the macro is stored. The second part (AddTotal or FormatFile) is the name of the procedure, taken from the procedure header.

QUICK TIP

If an error message appears, click Debug. Click the Reset button 🔳 on the toolbar, correct the error, then repeat Steps 6-8.

8. **Click** 'KHOT Procedures.xls'!AddTotal **to select it if necessary, then click** Run

   The AddTotal procedure inserts and formats the ad expenditure total in cell F18, as shown in Figure P-6.

9. **Save the workbook**

FIGURE P-5: VBA code for the AddTotal procedure

Save button

View Microsoft Excel button

New module name

In the xl terms, be sure to use a lowercase letter l, not the number 1

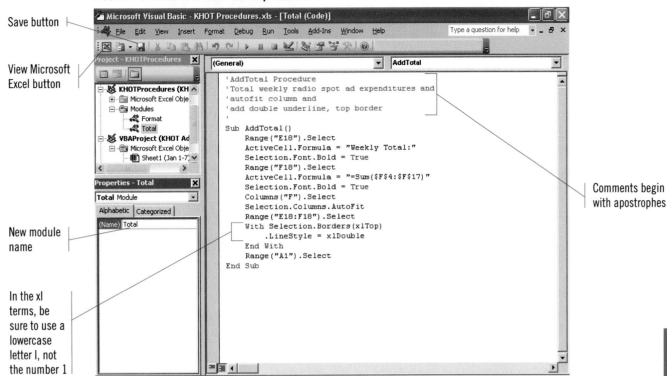

```
'AddTotal Procedure
'Total weekly radio spot ad expenditures and
'autofit column and
'add double underline, top border
'
Sub AddTotal()
    Range("E18").Select
    ActiveCell.Formula = "Weekly Total:"
    Selection.Font.Bold = True
    Range("F18").Select
    ActiveCell.Formula = "=Sum($F$4:$F$17)"
    Selection.Font.Bold = True
    Columns("F").Select
    Selection.Columns.AutoFit
    Range("E18:F18").Select
    With Selection.Borders(xlTop)
        .LineStyle = xlDouble
    End With
    Range("A1").Select
End Sub
```

Comments begin with apostrophes

FIGURE P-6: Worksheet after running the AddTotal procedure

Result of AddTotal procedure

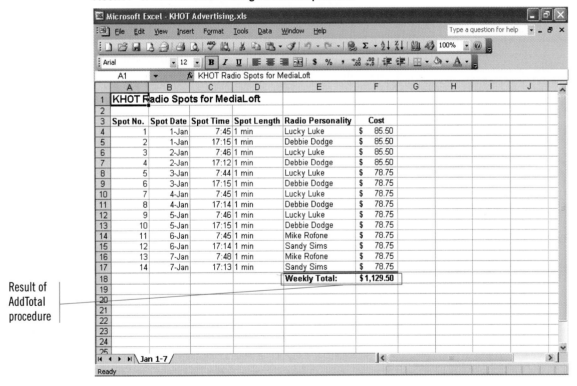

Clues to Use

Entering code using the scrollable word list

To assist you in entering the VBA code, the Editor often displays a list of words that can be used in the macro statement. Typically, the list appears after you press [.] (period). To include a word from the list in the macro statement, select the word in the list, then double click it or press [Tab]. For example, to enter the Range("E12").Select instruction, type Range(" E12"), then press [.] (period). Type s to bring up the words beginning with the letter s, select the Select command in the list, then press [Tab] to enter the word Select in the macro statement.

Adding a Conditional Statement

Sometimes, you may want a procedure to take an action based on a certain condition or set of conditions. For example, *if* a salesperson's performance rating is a 5 (top rating), *then* calculate a 10% bonus; otherwise (*else*), there is no bonus. One way of adding this type of conditional statement in Visual Basic is by using an **If...Then...Else statement**. The syntax for this statement is: "If *condition* Then *statements* Else [*else statements*]." The brackets indicate that the Else part of the statement is optional. ▰▰▰▰▰ Jim wants the worksheet to point out if the amount spent on radio ads stays within or exceeds the $1000 budget. You will use Excel to add a conditional statement that indicates this information. You start by returning to the Visual Basic Editor and inserting a new module in the KHOT Procedures project.

STEPS

QUICK TIP

You can also return to the Visual Basic Editor by clicking its button on the taskbar.

1. **With the Jan 1-7 worksheet still displayed, click Tools on the menu bar, point to Macro, click Visual Basic Editor, verify that KHOT Procedures is the active project in the Project Explorer window, click Insert on the Visual Basic Editor menu bar, then click Module**

   A new, blank module named Module1 is inserted in the KHOT Procedures workbook.

2. **In the Properties window click (Name), then type Budget**

3. **Click in the Code window, then type the code exactly as shown in Figure P-7**

   Notice the comment lines (in green) in the middle of the code. These lines help explain the procedure.

QUICK TIP

The If...Then...Else statement is similar to the Excel IF function.

4. **Compare the procedure you entered with Figure P-7; if necessary, make any corrections, click the Save KHOT Procedures.xls button 🖫 on the Visual Basic Editor Standard toolbar, then click the View Microsoft Excel button 🖾 on the toolbar**

5. **If necessary, click KHOT Advertising.xls in the taskbar to display it; with the Jan 1-7 worksheet displayed, click Tools on the menu bar, point to Macro, click Macros, in the Macro dialog box, click 'KHOT Procedures.xls'!BudgetStatus, then click Run**

   The BudgetStatus procedure indicates the status—over budget—as shown in Figure P-8.

6. **Save the workbook**

FIGURE P-7: VBA code for the BudgetStatus procedure

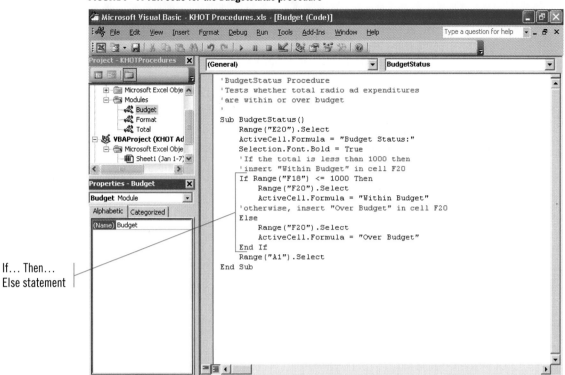

If... Then...
Else statement

```
'BudgetStatus Procedure
'Tests whether total radio ad expenditures
'are within or over budget
'
Sub BudgetStatus()
    Range("E20").Select
    ActiveCell.Formula = "Budget Status:"
    Selection.Font.Bold = True
    'If the total is less than 1000 then
    'insert "Within Budget" in cell F20
    If Range("F18") <= 1000 Then
        Range("F20").Select
        ActiveCell.Formula = "Within Budget"
    'otherwise, insert "Over Budget" in cell F20
    Else
        Range("F20").Select
        ActiveCell.Formula = "Over Budget"
    End If
    Range("A1").Select
End Sub
```

FIGURE P-8: Result of running the BudgetStatus procedure

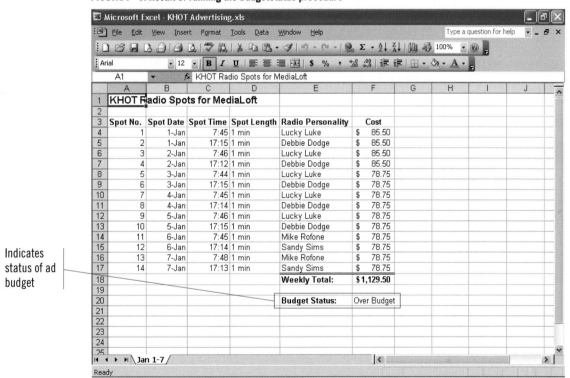

Indicates
status of ad
budget

Excel 2003

Prompting the User for Data

When automating routine tasks, you sometimes need to pause a macro to allow user input. You use the VBA InputBox function to display a dialog box that prompts the user for information. A **function** is a predefined procedure that returns (creates and displays) a value; in this case the value returned is the information the user enters. The required elements of an InputBox function are as follows: *object*.InputBox("*prompt*"), where "*prompt*" is the message that appears in the dialog box. For a detailed description of the InputBox function, use the Visual Basic Editor's Help menu. You decide to create a procedure that will insert the user's name in the left footer area of the workbook. You'll use the InputBox function to display a dialog box in which the user can enter his or her name. You will also type an error into the procedure code, which you will correct in the next lesson.

STEPS

1. **With the Jan 1-7 worksheet displayed, click** Tools **on the menu bar, point to** Macro, **click** Visual Basic Editor, **verify that KHOT Procedures is the active project, click** Insert **on the Visual Basic Editor menu bar, then click** Module

   A new, blank module named Module1 is inserted in the KHOT Procedures workbook.

2. **In the Properties window, click** (Name), **then type** Footer

QUICK TIP

To enlarge your Code window, place the mouse pointer on the left border of the Code window until it turns into ◄‖►, then drag the border to the left until the Code window is the desired size.

3. **Click in the Code window, then type the procedure code exactly as shown in Figure P-9**

   Like the Budget procedure, this procedure also contains comments that explain the code. The first part of the code, Dim LeftFooterText As String, **declares**, or defines, LeftFooterText as a text string variable. In Visual Basic, a **variable** is a location in memory in which you can temporarily store one item of information. Dim statements are used to declare variables and must be entered in the following format: Dim *variablename* As *datatype*. The datatype here is "string." In this case, you plan to store the information received from the input box in the temporary memory location called LeftFooterText. Then you can place this text in the left footer area. The remaining statements in the procedure are explained in the comment line directly above each statement. Notice the comment pointing out the error in the procedure code. You will correct this in the next lesson.

4. **Review your code, make any necessary changes, click the** Save KHOT Procedures.xls **button** 🖫 **on the Visual Basic Editor Standard toolbar, then click the** View Microsoft Excel **button** 🗏 **on the toolbar**

TROUBLE

If your macro doesn't prompt you for your name, it may contain a spelling or syntax error. Return to the Visual Basic Editor, click the Reset button 🔳, correct your error by referring to Figure P-9, then repeat Steps 4 and 5. You'll learn more about how to correct such macro errors in the next lesson.

5. **With the Jan 1-7 worksheet displayed, click** Tools **on the menu bar, point to** Macro, **click** Macros, **in the Macro dialog box click** 'KHOT Procedures.xls'!FooterInput, **then click** Run

   The procedure begins, and a dialog box generated by the InputBox function appears, prompting you to enter your name. See Figure P-10.

6. **With the cursor in the text box, type your name, then click** OK

7. **Click the** Print Preview button 🔍 **on the Standard toolbar**

   Although the customized footer with the date is inserted on the sheet, because of the error, your name does *not* appear in the left section of the footer. In the next lesson, you will learn how to step through a procedure's code line by line. This will help you locate the error in the FooterInput procedure.

8. **Click** Close **then save the workbook**

   You return to the Jan 1-7 worksheet.

FIGURE P-9: VBA code for the FooterInput procedure

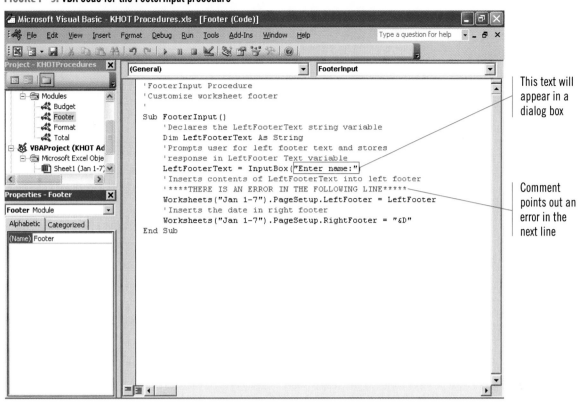

This text will appear in a dialog box

Comment points out an error in the next line

FIGURE P-10: InputBox function's dialog box

User prompt

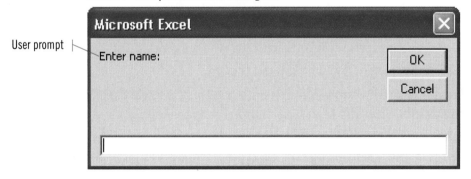

Excel 2003

Debugging a Macro

When a macro procedure does not run properly, it can be due to an error, referred to as a **bug**, in the code. To assist you in finding the bug(s) in a procedure, the Visual Basic Editor helps you step through the procedure's code, one line at a time. When you locate the error, you can then correct, or **debug**, it. 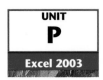 You decide to debug the macro procedure to find out why it failed to insert your name in the worksheet's footer.

STEPS

1. **With the KHOT Advertising Jan 1-7 worksheet displayed, click Tools on the menu bar, point to Macro, click Macros, in the Macro dialog box click 'KHOT Procedures.xls'!FooterInput, then click Step Into**

   The Visual Basic Editor appears with the statement selector positioned on the first statement of the procedure. See Figure P-11.

2. **Press [F8] to step to the next statement**

   The statement selector skips over the comments and the line of code beginning with Dim. The Dim statement indicates that the procedure will store your name in a variable named LeftFooterText. Because Dim is a declaration of a variable and not a procedure statement, the statement selector skips it and moves to the line containing the InputBox function.

3. **Press [F8] again; with the cursor in the text box in the Microsoft Excel dialog box, type your name, then click OK**

   The Visual Basic Editor reappears. The statement selector is now positioned on the statement that reads Worksheets ("Jan 1-7").PageSetup.LeftFooter = LeftFooter. This statement should insert your name (which you just typed in the text box) in the left section of the footer. This is the instruction that does not appear to be working correctly.

4. **If necessary, scroll right until the end of the LeftFooter instruction is visible, then place the mouse pointer Ⅰ on LeftFooter, as shown in Figure P-12**

   Rather than containing your name, the variable LeftFooter at the end of this line is empty. That's because the InputBox function assigned your name to the LeftFooterText variable, not to the LeftFooter variable. Before you can correct this bug, you need to turn off the Step Into feature.

5. **Click the Reset button 🔲 on the Visual Basic Editor toolbar to turn off the Step Into feature, click at the end of the statement containing the error, then replace the variable LeftFooter with LeftFooterText**

   The revised statement now reads Worksheets("Jan 1-7").PageSetup.LeftFooter = LeftFooterText.

6. **Delete the comment line pointing out the error**

7. **Click the Save KHOT Procedures.xls button 🔲 on the Visual Basic Editor Standard toolbar, then click the View Microsoft Excel button 🔲 on the toolbar**

8. **With the Jan 1-7 worksheet displayed, click Tools on the menu bar, point to Macro, click Macros; in the Macro dialog box, click 'KHOT Procedures.xls'!FooterInput, click Run to rerun the procedure, when prompted, type your name, then click OK**

9. **Click the Print Preview button 🔲 on the Standard toolbar**

   Your name now appears in the left section of the footer.

10. **Click Close, save the workbook, then print the worksheet**

FIGURE P-11: Statement selector positioned on first procedure statement

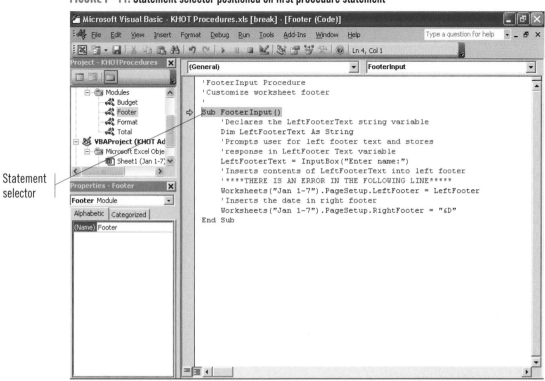

Statement
selector

FIGURE P-12: Value contained in LeftFooter variable

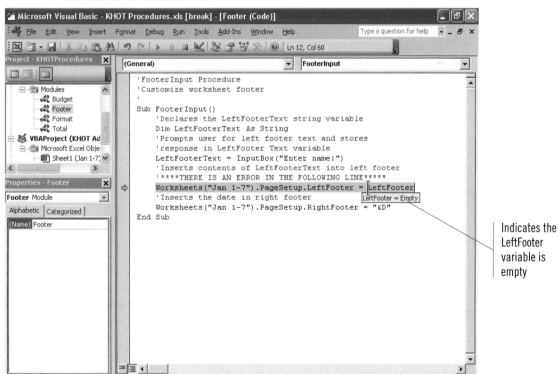

Indicates the
LeftFooter
variable is
empty

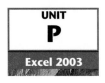

Creating a Main Procedure

When you routinely need to run several macros one after another, you can save time by combining them into one procedure. The resulting procedure, which processes (or runs) multiple procedures in sequence, is referred to as the **main procedure**. To create a main procedure, you type a Call statement for each procedure you want to run. The syntax of the Call statement is Call *procedurename*, where *procedurename* is the name of the procedure you want to run. To avoid having to run his macros one after another every month, Jim asks you to create a main procedure that will run (or call) each of the procedures in the KHOT Procedures workbook in sequence.

STEPS

1. **With the Jan 1-7 worksheet displayed, click Tools on the menu bar, point to Macro, then click Visual Basic Editor**

2. **Verify that KHOT Procedures is the active project, click Insert on the menu bar, then click Module**

   A new, blank module named Module1 is inserted in the KHOT Procedures workbook.

3. **In the Properties window, click (Name), then type MainProc**

4. **In the Code window, enter the procedure code exactly as shown in Figure P-13**

5. **Compare your main procedure code with Figure P-13, correct any errors, if necessary, then click the Save KHOT Procedures.xls button on the Visual Basic Editor Standard toolbar**

   To test the new main procedure you need an unformatted version of the KHOT radio spot workbook.

6. **Click the View Microsoft Excel button on the toolbar, then close the KHOT Advertising workbook**

   The KHOT Procedures workbook remains open.

7. **Open the Data File titled EX P-2.xls from the drive and folder where your Data Files are stored, then save it as KHOT Advertising 2**

   In the next lesson, you'll run the main procedure.

FIGURE P-13: VBA code for the MainProcedure procedure

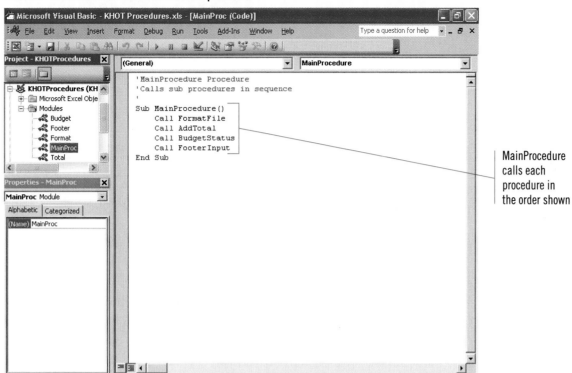

MainProcedure calls each procedure in the order shown

Excel 2003

Running a Main Procedure

Running a main procedure allows you to run several macros in sequence. You can run a main procedure just as you would any other macro procedure—by selecting it in the Macro dialog box, then clicking Run. You have finished creating Jim's main procedure, and you are ready to run it. If the main procedure works correctly, it should format the worksheet, insert the ad expenditure total, insert a budget status message, and add your name to the worksheet footer.

STEPS

QUICK TIP
You can run a macro using a shortcut key combination by clicking the Options button in the Macro dialog box and entering the key combination that runs the macro.

1. **With the Jan 1-7 worksheet displayed, click Tools on the menu bar, point to Macro, then click Macros; in the Macro dialog box, click 'KHOT Procedures.xls'!MainProcedure, click Run, when prompted, type your name, then click OK**

   The MainProcedure runs the FormatFile, AddTotal, BudgetStatus, and FooterInput procedures in sequence. You can see the results of the FormatFile, AddTotal, and BudgetStatus procedures in the worksheet window. See Figure P-14. To view the results of the FooterInput procedure, you need to switch to the Preview window.

2. **Click the Print Preview button 🔍 on the Standard toolbar, verify that your name appears in the left footer area and the date appears in the right footer area, then click Close**

3. **Click Tools on the menu bar, point to Macro, then click Visual Basic Editor**

   You decide to add your name to each procedure.

4. **In the Project Explorer window, double-click each module and add a comment line after the procedure name that reads Written by [your name], then click the Save KHOT Procedures.xls button 🖫 on the toolbar**

5. **Click File on the Visual Basic Editor menu bar, then click Print**

   The Print - KHOTProcedures dialog box opens, as shown in Figure P-15. You could print each procedure separately, but it's faster to print all the procedures in the workbook at one time. Recall that all procedures in a workbook are known as a project.

6. **In the Print - KHOTProcedures dialog box, click the Current Project option button, then click OK**

   Each procedure prints on a separate page.

7. **Click the View Microsoft Excel button 🔲 on the toolbar**

QUICK TIP
You can run a macro from a button on your worksheet. Create a button using the rectangle tool or an AutoShape on the drawing toolbar, select the button, then right-click one of the button's edges and choose Assign Macro to choose the macro the button will run.

8. **Save the KHOT Advertising 2 workbook and close it; close the KHOT Procedures workbook, then exit Excel**

FIGURE P-14: Result of running MainProcedure procedure

Total cost calculated

Budget status message inserted

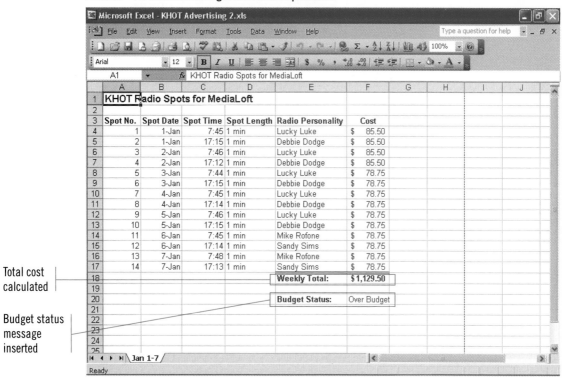

FIGURE P-15: Printing the macro procedures

Current Project option button

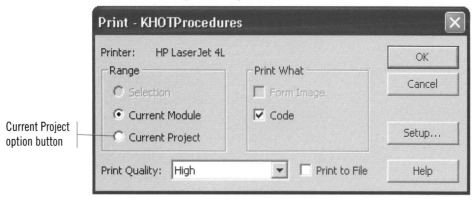

Practice

▼ CONCEPTS REVIEW

FIGURE P-16

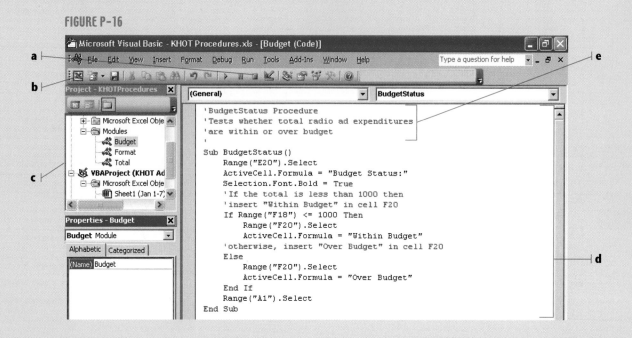

1. **Which element do you click to turn off the Step Into feature?**
2. **Which element do you click to return to Excel from the Visual Basic Editor?**
3. **Which element points to the Project Explorer window?**
4. **Which element points to the Code window?**
5. **Which element points to comments in the VBA code?**

Match each term with the statement that best describes it.

6. **Keywords**
7. **Comments**
8. **Procedure**
9. **Sub procedure**
10. **Function**

a. Another term for a macro in Visual Basic for Applications (VBA)
b. A procedure that returns a value
c. Words that are recognized as part of the programming language
d. A series of statements that perform an action but don't return a value
e. Descriptive text used to explain parts of a procedure

Select the best answer from the list of choices.

11. **A location in memory where you can temporarily store information is a(n):**
   a. Function
   b. Procedure
   c. Sub procedure
   d. Variable

12. You enter the statements of a macro in:
- **a.** The Macro dialog box
- **b.** The Code window of the Visual Basic Editor
- **c.** The Properties window of the Visual Basic Editor
- **d.** Any blank worksheet

13. If your macro doesn't run correctly, you should:
- **a.** Create an If...Then...Else statement.
- **b.** Click the Properties button.
- **d.** Click the Project Explorer button.
- **c.** Select the macro in the Macro dialog box, click Step Into, and then debug the macro.

14. Comments are displayed in _____ in VBA code.
- **a.** Green
- **b.** Blue
- **c.** Red
- **d.** Black

15. Keywords are displayed in _____ in VBA code.
- **a.** Red
- **b.** Black
- **c.** Green
- **d.** Blue

▼ SKILLS REVIEW

1. View and analyze VBA code.
- **a.** Start Excel, open the Data File titled EX P-3.xls from the drive and folder where your Data Files are stored, enable macros, then save it as **Northeast Sales**.
- **b.** Review the unformatted January 2006 worksheet.
- **c.** Open the Visual Basic Editor.
- **d.** Select the ListFormat module and review the FormatList procedure.
- **e.** Insert comments in the procedure code describing what action you think each line of code will perform. (*Hint*: One of the statements will sort the list alphabetically by city.)
- **f.** Save the macro, return to the worksheet, then run the FormatList macro.
- **g.** Compare the results with the code and your comments.
- **h.** Save the workbook.

2. Write VBA code.
- **a.** Open the Visual Basic Editor and insert a new module named **Total** in the Northeast Sales project.
- **b.** Enter the code for the SalesTotal procedure exactly as shown in Figure P-17.
- **c.** Save the macro.
- **d.** Return to the January 2006 worksheet and run the SalesTotal macro.
- **e.** Save the workbook.

FIGURE P-17

```
'SalesTotal Procedure
'Totals January sales
Sub SalesTotal()
    Range("E17").Select
    ActiveCell.Formula = "=SUM($E$3:$E$16)"
    Selection.Font.Bold = True
    With Selection.Borders(xlTop)
        .LineStyle = xlSingle
    End With
    Range("A1").Select
End Sub
```

3. Add a conditional statement.
- **a.** Open the Visual Basic Editor and insert a new module named **Goal** in the Northeast Sales project.
- **b.** Enter the SalesGoal procedure exactly as shown in Figure P-18.
- **c.** Save the macro.
- **d.** Return to the January 2006 worksheet and run the SalesGoal macro. The procedure should enter the message **Missed goal** in cell E18.
- **e.** Save the workbook.

FIGURE P-18

```
'SalesGoal Procedure
'Tests whether sales goal was met
Sub SalesGoal()
    'If the total is >=185000, then insert "Met Goal"
    'in cell E18
    If Range("E17") >= 185000 Then
        Range("E18").Select
        ActiveCell.Formula = "Met goal"
    'otherwise, insert "Missed goal" in cell E18
    Else
        Range("E18").Select
        ActiveCell.Formula = "Missed goal"
    End If
End Sub
```

▼ SKILLS REVIEW (CONTINUED)

4. **Prompt the user for data.**

   a. Open the Visual Basic Editor and insert a new module named **Header** in the Northeast Sales project.

   b. Enter the HeaderFooter procedure exactly as shown in Figure P-19. You will be entering an error in the procedure that will be corrected in Step 5.

   c. Save the macro then return to the January 2006 worksheet and run the HeaderFooter macro.

   d. Preview the January 2006 worksheet. Your name should be missing from the left section of the footer.

   e. Save the workbook.

FIGURE P-19

```
'HeaderFooter Procedure
'Procedure to customize the header and footer
Sub HeaderFooter()
    'Inserts the filename in the header
    Worksheets("January 2006").PageSetup.CenterHeader = "&F"
    'Declares the variable LeftFooterText as a string
    Dim LeftFooterText As String
    'Prompts user for left footer text
    LeftFooter = InputBox("Enter your full name:")
    'Inserts response into left footer
    Worksheets("January 2006").PageSetup.LeftFooter = LeftFooterText
    'Inserts the date into right footer
    Worksheets("January 2006").PageSetup.RightFooter = "&D"
End Sub
```

5. **Debug a macro.**

   a. Open the Visual Basic Editor.

   b. The error occurs on the line:

   LeftFooter = InputBox("Enter your full name:")

   (The variable that will input the response text into the worksheet footer is LeftFooterText.)

   c. Correct the error by changing the line with the error to:

   LeftFooterText = InputBox("Enter your full name:")

   d. Save the macro, then return to the January 2006 worksheet and run the HeaderFooter macro again.

   e. Verify that your name now appears in the left section of the footer.

   f. Save the workbook.

6. **Create and run a main procedure.**

   a. Return to the Visual Basic Editor, insert a new module, then name it **MainProc**.

   b. Begin the main procedure by entering comments in the code window that provide the procedure's name (MainProcedure) and explain that its purpose is to run the FormatList, SalesTotal, SalesGoal, and HeaderFooter procedures.

   c. Enter the procedure header: **Sub MainProcedure()**.

   d. Enter four Call statements that will run the FormatList, SalesTotal, SalesGoal, and HeaderFooter procedures in sequence.

   e. Save the procedure and return to Excel.

   f. Open the EX P-3.xls workbook, then save it as Northeast Sales 2.

   g. Run the MainProcedure macro, entering your name when prompted. (*Hint*: In the Macro dialog box, the macro procedures you created will now have 'Northeast Sales.xls'! as part of their names. That's because the macros are stored in the Northeast Sales workbook, not in the Northeast Sales 2 workbook.)

   h. Verify that the macro ran successfully, save the Northeast Sales 2 workbook, print the January 2006 worksheet, then close the Northeast Sales 2 workbook.

   i. Return to the Visual Basic Editor, enter your name in a comment line in each procedure, print the current project's code, then close the Visual Basic Editor.

   j. Return to Excel, close the Northeast Sales workbook, then exit Excel.

▼ INDEPENDENT CHALLENGE 1

You work at an art supply store. Your coworker is on vacation for two weeks, and you have taken over her projects. The information systems manager asks you to document and test the Excel procedure Qtr1, which your coworker wrote for the company's accountant. You will run the macro procedure first to see what it does, then you will add comments to the VBA code to document it. Lastly, you will enter data to verify that the formulas in the macro work correctly.

▼ INDEPENDENT CHALLENGE 1 (CONTINUED)

a. Start Excel, open the Data File titled EX P-4.xls from the drive and folder where your Data Files are stored, enable macros, then save it as **First Quarter Income**.

b. Run the Qtr1 macro, noting anything that you think should be mentioned in your documentation.

c. Review the Qtr1 procedure in the Visual Basic Editor. It is stored in the Quarter 1 module.

d. Document the procedure by annotating the printed code, indicating the actions the procedure performs and the objects (ranges) that are affected. (*Hint*: The month names are entered into cells B1, C1, and D1. The income row headers are entered into cells A2, A4, A5, and A6. The Total Income header is entered into cell A8. The column headers are bolded. The row headers are bolded. Columns A through D are AutoFitted. Totals are entered into cells B8, C8, and D8.)

e. Enter your name in a comment line.

f. Save the procedure, then print the procedure code.

g. Return to the First Quarter Income workbook and use Figure P-20 as a guide to enter data in cells B4:D6 of Sheet1. The totals will be displayed as you enter the income data.

h. Check the total income calculations in row 8 to verify that the macro is working correctly.

i. Enter your name in the Sheet1 footer, save the worksheet, then print the worksheet.

j. Close the workbook, then exit Excel.

FIGURE P-20

	A	B	C	D	E
1		January	Feburary	March	
2	Income				
3					
4	Supplies	600	500	480	
5	Classes	800	675	650	
6	Consulting	300	700	900	
7					
8	Total Income				

▼ INDEPENDENT CHALLENGE 2

You work in the sales office of an automobile dealership called Team Motors. Each month you are required to produce a report stating whether sales quotas were met for the following three vehicle categories: compacts, sedans, and sports/utility. This quarter, the sales quotas for each month are as follows: compacts 65, sedans 50, and sports/utility 65. The results this month were 45, 65, and 75, respectively. You decide to create a procedure to automate your monthly task of determining the sales quota status for the vehicle categories. You would like your assistant to take this task over when you go on vacation next month. Because he has no previous experience with Excel, you decide to create a second procedure that prompts a user with input boxes to enter the actual sales results for the month.

a. Start Excel, open the Data File titled EX P-5.xls from the drive and folder where your Data Files are stored, then save it as **Sales Quota Status**.

b. Use the Visual Basic Editor to insert a new module named **Quotas** in the Sales Quota Status workbook. Create a procedure in the new module named **SalesQuota** that determines the sales quota status for each vehicle category and enters Yes or No in the Status column. The VBA code is shown in Figure P-21.

c. Add comments to document the SalesQuota procedure, including your name, then save it.

FIGURE P-21

```
Sub SalesQuota()

    If Range("C4") >= 65 Then
        Range("D4").Select
        ActiveCell.Formula = "Yes"
    Else
        Range("D4").Select
        ActiveCell.Formula = "No"
    End If

    If Range("C5") >= 50 Then
        Range("D5").Select
        ActiveCell.Formula = "Yes"
    Else
        Range("D5").Select
        ActiveCell.Formula = "No"
    End If

    If Range("C6") >= 65 Then
        Range("D6").Select
        ActiveCell.Formula = "Yes"
    Else
        Range("D6").Select
        ActiveCell.Formula = "No"
    End If

End Sub
```

▼ INDEPENDENT CHALLENGE 2 (CONTINUED)

d. Insert a new module named **MonthlySales**. Create a second procedure named **Sales** that prompts a user for sales data for each vehicle category, enters the input data in the appropriate cells, then calls the SalesQuota procedure. The VBA code is shown in Figure P-22.

e. Insert your name in a **Created by** comment below the procedure name. Enter comments to document the macro actions. Save the procedure.

f. Run the Sales macro and enter 45 for compact sales, 65 for sedan sales, and 75 for sports/utility sales. Correct any errors in the VBA code.

g. Print the current project's code, then return to the workbook.

Advanced Challenge Exercise

- Assign a shortcut of [Ctrl][w] to the Sales macro. Insert a line on the worksheet that tells the user to press [Ctrl][w] to enter sales data.
- Delete the data in cells C4:D6.
- Run the macro using the shortcut key combination entering 70 for compact sales, 30 for sedan sales, and 60 for sports/utility sales.

FIGURE P-22

```
Sub Sales()

    Dim Compact As String
    Compact = InputBox("Enter Compact Sales")
    Range("C4").Select
    Selection = Compact

    Dim Sedans As String
    Sedans = InputBox("Enter Sedan Sales")
    Range("C5").Select
    Selection = Sedans

    Dim SportsUtility As String
    SportsUtility = InputBox("Enter SportsUtility Sales")
    Range("C6").Select
    Selection = SportsUtility

    Call SalesQuota

End Sub
```

h. Add your name to the left section of the worksheet footer, save the workbook, then print the worksheet. Close the workbook, then exit Excel.

▼ INDEPENDENT CHALLENGE 3

You own a flower store named Tulips. You have started to advertise your business using a local magazine, billboards, cable TV, radio, and local newspapers. Every month you prepare a report with the advertising expenses detailed by source. You decide to create a macro that will format the monthly reports. You add the same footers on every report, so you will create another macro that will add a footer to a document. Finally, you will create a main procedure that will call the macros to format the report and add a footer. You begin by creating a workbook with data you can use to test the macros. You will save the macros you create in this workbook.

a. Use Figure P-23 as a guide to create a workbook containing the January advertising expenses. Save the workbook as **Tulips** in the drive and folder where your Data Files are stored.

FIGURE P-23

	A	B	C	D	E	F	G
1	Tulips						
2	Ad Campaign						
3	Advertising Type	Source	Cost				
4	Magazine	What's Happening	500				
5	Newspaper	Times	450				
6	Billboard	First Street	550				
7	TV	Cable TV	300				
8	Radio	Public Radio	550				
9							

b. Insert a module named **Format**, then create a procedure named Formatting that:
- Selects a cell in row 3 and inserts a row in the worksheet above it
- Selects the cost data in column C and formats it as currency. (Hint: After the row is inserted, this range is C5:C9.)
- Selects cell A1 before ending

▼ INDEPENDENT CHALLENGE 3 (CONTINUED)

    c. Save the Formatting procedure.

    d. Insert a module named **Foot**, then create a procedure named Footer that:

- Declares a string variable for text that will be placed in the left footer
- Uses an input box to prompt the user for his or her name and places the name in the left footer
- Places the date in the right footer

    e. Save the Footer procedure.

    f. Insert a module named **Main**, then create a procedure named MainProc that calls the new Footer procedure and the Formatting procedure.

    g. Save your work, then run the MainProc procedure. Debug each procedure as necessary.

    h. Insert your name in a comment line under each procedure name, then print the code for the current project.

    i. Return to the January worksheet, save the workbook, then print the worksheet.

    j. Close the workbook, then exit Excel.

▼ INDEPENDENT CHALLENGE 4

You are working as an assistant currency trader for an international bank based in London. To keep on top of the fluctuating world currencies, you create a daily report using data imported from the Web to an Excel spreadsheet. Since you perform the same formatting and place the same header and footer on each report, you decide to write a macro that will do this automatically.

    a. Start Excel, create a new workbook, then save it as **Currency Rates** in the drive and folder where your Data Files are stored.

    b. Use the search engine of your choice to search for world currency rates. Find a Web site that displays the rate information in a table.

    c. Copy the currency rate information from the Web page into Sheet1 of your Currency Rates workbook, then save the workbook.

    d. Use the Visual Basic Editor to create a procedure named Formatting that does the following:

- Inserts a blank row after the column headers
- Changes the font size of the column and row headers to 14
- Bolds the currency data
- Adds a footer with your name in the left section and the date in the right section

    e. Enter your name as a comment in the procedure.

    f. Save your work, then return to the worksheet and test the new macro.

    g. Debug the macro as necessary, print the module, then close the Visual Basic Editor.

    h. Return to the Currency Rates workbook, then resize the columns on Sheet1 as necessary. Save the workbook, then print the worksheet.

FIGURE P-24

Advanced Challenge Exercise

- Use the Visual Basic Editor to create a procedure named Printdata that prints a worksheet. Use Figure P-24 as a guide. Note that your range depends on the amount of data on your worksheet.

```
Sub Printdata()

'Your range will be different on the next two lines

Range("A1:C17").Select
ActiveSheet.PageSetup.PrintArea = "$A$1:$C$17"
ActiveWindow.SelectedSheets.PrintOut Copies:=1

End Sub
```

- Save the macro and return to the worksheet.
- Assign the macro Printdata to a button on the worksheet. (*Hint*: Use the Rectangle tool to create the button, label the button **Print**, select the button and then right-click one of the button's edges to assign the macro.)
- Test the button.

    i. Save the workbook, close the workbook, then exit Excel.

▼ VISUAL WORKSHOP

Open the Data File titled EX P-6.xls and save it as **Strings** in the drive and folder where your Data Files are stored. Create a macro procedure that will format the worksheet as shown in Figure P-25. Run the macro and debug it as necessary to make the worksheet match Figure P-25. Insert your name in a comment line under the procedure name, then print the procedure code.

FIGURE P-25

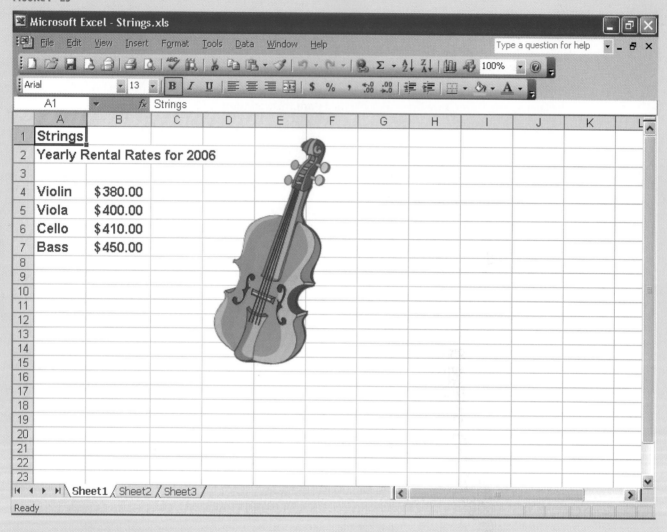

Glossary

3-D reference A reference that uses values on other sheets or workbooks, effectively creating another dimension to a workbook.

Absolute cell reference A cell reference that contains a dollar sign before the column letter and/or row number to indicate the absolute, or fixed, contents of specific cells. For example, the formula $A$1+$B$1 calculates only the sum of these specific cells no matter where the formula is copied in the workbook.

Active cell The current location of the cell pointer.

Alignment The placement of cell contents; for example, left, center, or right.

Analyze To manipulate data, such as a list, with Excel or another tool.

AND condition A filtering feature that searches for records by specifying that all entered criteria must be matched.

Apply To open a document based on an Excel template.

Area chart A line chart in which each area is given a solid color or pattern to emphasize the relationship between the pieces of charted information.

Argument Information that a function needs to calculate an answer. In an expression, multiple arguments are separated by commas. All of the arguments are enclosed in parentheses; for example, =SUM(A1:B1).

Argument ScreenTip The yellow box that appears as you build a function. As you build the function using different elements, the box displays these elements. You can click each element to display its online help.

Arithmetic operator A symbol used in a formula (such as + or -, /, or *) to perform mathematical operations.

ASCII file A text file that contains data but no formatting; instead of being divided into columns, ASCII file data are separated, or delimited, by tabs or commas.

Ascending order In sorting worksheet records, the order that begins with the letter A or the number 1.

Attribute The styling features such as bold, italics, and underlining that can be applied to cell contents. In XML, the component that provides information about the document's elements.

Auditing An Excel feature that helps track errors and check worksheet logic.

AutoCalculate value Value displayed in the status bar that represents the sum of values in the selected range.

AutoComplete A feature that automatically completes entries based on other entries in the same column.

AutoFill A feature that creates a series of text entries or numbers when a range is selected using the fill handle.

AutoFill Options button Allows you to specify what you want to fill and whether or not you want to include formatting.

AutoFilter An Excel list feature that lets you click a list arrow and select criteria by which to display certain types of records.

AutoFilter list arrows Small triangles that appear next to field names in an Excel list; used to display portions of your data.

AutoFit A feature that automatically adjusts the width of a column to accommodate its widest entry when the boundary to the right of the column selector is double-clicked.

AutoFormat Preset schemes that can be applied to format a range instantly. Excel comes with 16 AutoFormats that include colors, fonts, and numeric formatting.

AutoSum A feature that automatically creates totals using the SUM function when you click the AutoSum button.

Background color The color applied to the background of a cell.

Backsolving A problem-solving method in which you specify a solution and then find the input value that produces the answer you want; sometimes described as a what-if analysis in reverse. In Excel, the Goal Seek feature performs backsolving.

Bar chart A chart that shows information as a series of horizontal bars.

Border The edge of a cell, an area of a worksheet, or a selected object; you can change its color or line style.

Bug In programming, an error that causes a procedure to run incorrectly.

Category axis The x-axis (horizontal axis) of a chart.

Cell The intersection of a column and row in a worksheet, datasheet, or table.

Cell address The location of a cell expressed by the column and row coordinates; the cell address of the cell in column A, row 1, is A1.

Cell comments Notes you've written about a workbook that appear when you place the pointer over a cell.

Cell pointer A highlighted rectangle around a cell that indicates the active cell.

Cell reference The address or name that identifies a cell's position in a worksheet; it consists of a letter that identifies the cell's column and a number that identifies its row; for example, cell B3. Cell references in worksheets can be used in formulas and are relative or absolute. *See also* Absolute cell reference and Relative cell reference.

Change history A worksheet containing a list of changes made to a shared workbook.

Changing cells In what-if analysis, cells that contain the values that change in order to produce multiple sets of results.

Chart A graphic representation of worksheet information. Types include 2-D and 3-D column, bar, pie, area, and line charts.

Chart sheet A separate sheet that contains only a chart linked to worksheet data.

Chart Wizard A series of dialog boxes that helps you create or modify a chart.

Clip An individual media file, such as art, sound, animation, or a movie.

Clip art An image such as a corporate logo, a picture, or a photo.

Clipboard A temporary storage area for cut or copied items that are available for pasting. *See also* Office Clipboard.

Clipboard task pane A task pane that shows the contents of the Office Clipboard; contains options for copying and pasting items.

Code *See* Program Code.

Code window In the Visual Basic Editor, the window that displays the selected module's procedures, written in the Visual Basic programming language.

Column chart The default chart type in Excel, which displays information as a series of vertical columns.

Column heading The gray box containing the letter above the column in a worksheet.

Combination chart Combines a column and line chart to compare data requiring different scales of measure.

Comments In a Visual Basic procedure, notes that explain the purpose of the macro or procedure; they are preceded by a single apostrophe and appear in green. *See also* cell comments.

Complex formula An equation that uses more than one type of arithmetic operator.

Conditional format A cell format that is based on the cell's value or the outcome of a formula.

Conditional formula A formula that makes calculations based on stated conditions, such as calculating a rebate based on a particular purchase amount.

Consolidate To combine data on multiple worksheets and display the result on another worksheet.

Control menu box A box in the upper-left corner of a window used to resize or close a window.

Criteria Conditions that must be met when searching for files.

Criteria range A cell range containing one row of labels (usually a copy of column labels) and at least one additional row underneath it that contains the criteria you want to match.

Custom chart type A specially formatted Excel chart.

Data entry area The unlocked portion of a worksheet where users are able to enter and change data.

Data form In an Excel list (or database), a dialog box that displays one record at a time.

Data label Descriptive text that appears above a data marker in a chart.

Data marker A graphical representation of a data point, such as a bar or column.

Data point Individual piece of data plotted in a chart.

Data series The selected range in a worksheet that Excel converts into a graphic and displays as a chart.

Data table A range of cells that shows the resulting values when one or more input values are varied in a formula; when one input value is changed, the table is called a one-input data table, and when two input values are changed, it is called a two-input data table. In a chart it is a grid containing the chart data.

Data validation A feature that allows you to specify what data is allowable (valid) for a range of cells.

Database An organized collection of related information. In Excel, a database is called a list.

Debug In programming, to find and correct an error in code.

Declare In the Visual Basic programming language, assigning a type, such as numeric or text, to a variable.

Delimiter A tab or space used in text files to separate columns of data.

Dependent cell A cell, usually containing a formula, whose value changes depending on the values in the input cells. For example, a payment formula or function that depends on an input cell containing changing interest rates is a dependent cell.

Descending order In sorting an Excel list, the order that begins with the letter Z or the highest number in a list.

Destination program In a data exchange, the program that will receive the data.

Document To make notes about basic worksheet assumptions, complex formulas, or questionable data. In a macro, to insert comments that explain the Visual Basic code.

Drag-and-drop technique Method in which you drag the contents of selected cells to a new location.

Dummy column/row Blank column or row included at the end of a range that enables a formula to adjust when columns or rows are added or deleted.

Dynamic page breaks In a larger workbook, horizontal or vertical dashed lines that represent the place where pages print separately. They also adjust automatically when you insert or delete rows or columns, or change column widths or row heights.

Electronic spreadsheet A computer program that performs calculations on data and organizes information into worksheets. A worksheet is divided into columns and rows, which form individual cells.

Element An XML component that defines the document content.

Embedded chart A chart displayed as an object in a worksheet.

Embedding Inserting a copy of data into a destination document; you can double-click the embedded object to modify it using the tools of the source program.

Exploding pie slice A slice of a pie chart that has been pulled away from the whole pie to add emphasis.

Extensible Markup Language (XML) A system for defining languages using tags to structure data.

External reference indicator The exclamation point (!) used in a formula to indicate that a referenced cell is outside the active sheet.

Extract To place a copy of a filtered list in a range you specify in the Advanced Filter dialog box.

Field In a list (an Excel database), a column that describes a characteristic about records, such as first name or city.

Field name A column label that describes a field.

File properties Attributes of a file, such as author name, file size, and file type.

Fill color The cell background color.

Fill handle A small square in the lower-right corner of the active cell used to copy cell contents.

Filter To display data in an Excel list that meet specified criteria.

Font The typeface or design of a set of characters.

Font size The size of characters, measured in units called points (pts).

Footer Information that prints at the bottom of each printed page; on screen, a footer is visible only in Print Preview.

Format The appearance of text and numbers, including color, font, attributes, borders, and shading. *See also* Number format.

Format Painter A feature used to copy the formatting applied to one set of text or in one cell to another.

Formatting toolbar A toolbar that contains buttons for frequently used formatting commands.

Formula A set of instructions used to perform numeric calculations (adding, multiplying, averaging, etc.).

Formula bar The area below the menu bar and above the Excel workspace where you enter and edit data in a worksheet cell. The formula bar becomes active when you start typing or editing cell data. It includes the Enter button and the Cancel button.

Formula prefix An arithmetic symbol, such as the equal sign (=), used to start a formula.

Freeze To hold in place selected columns or rows when scrolling in a worksheet that is divided in panes. *See also* panes.

Function A special, predefined formula that provides a shortcut for a commonly used calculation; for example, AVERAGE.

Getting Started task pane Lets you quickly open new or existing workbooks.

Goal cell In backsolving, a cell containing a formula in which you can substitute values to find a specific value, or goal.

Goal Seek A problem-solving method in which you specify a solution and then find the input value that produces the answer you want; sometimes described as a what-if analysis in reverse; also called backsolving.

Gridlines Horizontal and/or vertical lines within a chart that make the chart easier to read.

Header Information that prints at the top of each printed page; on screen, a header is visible only in Print Preview.

Help system A utility that gives you immediate access to definitions, steps, explanations, and useful tips.

Hide To make rows, columns, formulas, or sheets invisible to workbook users.

Hotspot An object that, when clicked, will run a macro or open a file.

HTML Hypertext Markup Language, the format of pages that a Web browser such as Internet Explorer or Netscape Navigator can read.

Hyperlink An object (a filename, a word, a phrase, or a graphic) in a worksheet that, when you click it, will display another worksheet or a Web page called the target.

If...Then...Else statement In the Visual Basic programming language, a conditional statement that directs Excel to perform specified actions under certain conditions; its syntax is "If *condition* Then *statements* Else [*elsestatements*]".

Input Information that produces desired results, or output, in a worksheet.

Input cells Spreadsheet cells that contain data instead of formulas and that act as input to a what-if analysis; input values often change to produce different results. Examples include interest rates, prices, or other data.

Insert row The last row in an Excel list, where a record can be entered.

Insertion point The blinking vertical line that appears in the formula bar or in a cell during editing in Excel.

Integration A process where data is exchanged among Excel and other Windows programs; can include pasting, importing, exporting, embedding, and linking.

Interactivity A feature of a worksheet saved as an HTML document and posted to an intranet or Web site that allows users to manipulate data using their browsers.

Intranet An internal network site used by a particular group of people who work together.

Keyword A representative word on which the Help system can search to find information on your area of interest. In a macro procedure, words that are recognized as part of the Visual Basic programming language.

Label Descriptive text or other information that identifies the rows and columns of a worksheet. Labels are not included in calculations.

Label prefix A character, such as the apostrophe, that identifies an entry as a label and controls the way it appears in the cell.

Landscape orientation A print setting that positions the worksheet on the page so the page is wider than it is tall.

Legend A key explaining how information is represented by colors or patterns in a chart.

Line chart A graph of data that is mapped by a series of lines. Line charts show changes in data or categories of data over time and can be used to document trends.

Linking Inserting an object into a destination program; The information you insert will be updated automatically when the data in the source document changes.

List The Excel term for a database, an organized collection of related information.

Lock To secure a row, column, or sheet so that data in that location cannot be changed.

Logical condition A filtering feature that searches for records using And and Or conditions; the conditions can include operators such as greater than or less than.

Logical test The first part of an IF function; if the logical test is true, then the second part of the function is applied, and if it is false, then the third part of the function is applied.

Macro A set of instructions recorded or written in the Visual Basic programming language used to automate worksheet tasks.

Main procedure A procedure containing several macros that run sequentially.

Manual calculation option An option that turns off automatic calculation of worksheet formulas, allowing you to selectively determine if and when you want Excel to perform calculations.

Map An XML schema that is attached to a workbook.

Map an XML element A process where XML element names are placed on an Excel worksheet in a specific locations.

Menu bar The bar beneath the title bar that contains the names of menus, that when clicked, open menus from which you choose program commands.

Minor gridlines Gridlines that show the values between the tick marks.

Mixed reference A formula containing both a relative and absolute reference.

Mode indicator A box located in the lower-left corner of the status bar that informs you of a program's status. For example, when Excel is performing a task, the word "Wait" appears.

Model A worksheet used to produce a what-if analysis that acts as the basis for multiple outcomes.

Module In Visual Basic, a module is stored in a workbook and contains macro procedures.

Moving border The dashed line that appears around a cell or range that is copied to the Clipboard.

Name box The left-most area in the formula bar that shows the cell reference or name of the active cell. For example, A1 refers to cell A1 of the active worksheet. You can also display a list of names in a workbook using the Name list arrow.

Named range A range of cells given a meaningful name; it retains its name when moved and can be referenced in a formula.

Number format A format applied to values to express numeric concepts, such as currency, date, and percentage.

Object A chart or graphic image that can be moved and resized and contains handles when selected. In object linking and embedding (OLE), the data to be exchanged between another document or program. In Visual Basic, every Excel element, including ranges.

Object Linking and Embedding (OLE) A Microsoft Windows technology that allows you to transfer data from one document and program to another using embedding or linking.

Office Clipboard A temporary storage area shared by all Office programs that can be used to cut, copy and paste multiple items within and between Office programs. The Office Clipboard can hold up to 24 items collected from any Office program. *See also* Clipboard and Clipboard task pane.

OLE *See* Object Linking and Embedding.

One-input data table A range of cells that shows resulting values when one input value in a formula is changed.

Order of precedence The order in which Excel calculates parts of a formula: (1) operations in parentheses (2) exponents, (3) multiplication and division, and (4) addition and subtraction.

Outline symbols In outline view, the buttons that, when clicked, changes the amount of detail in the outlined worksheet.

Output The end result of a worksheet.

Page field In a PivotTable or a PivotChart report, a field area that lets you view data as if it is stacked in pages, effectively adding a third dimension to the data analysis.

Panes Sections into which you can divide a worksheet when you want to work on separate parts of the worksheet at the same time; one pane freezes, or remains in place, while you scroll in another pane until you see the desired information.

Paste Function A series of dialog boxes that helps you build functions; it lists and describes all Excel functions.

Personal macro workbook A workbook that can contain macros that are available to any open workbook. By default, the personal macro workbook is hidden.

Pie chart A circular chart that represents data as slices of a pie. A pie chart is useful for showing the relationship of parts to a whole; pie slices can be extracted for emphasis. *See also* Exploding pie slice.

PivotChart report An Excel feature that lets you summarize worksheet data in the form of a chart in which you can rearrange, or "pivot," parts of the chart structure to explore new data relationships.

PivotTable Field List A window containing fields that can be used to create or modify a PivotTable.

PivotTable list An interactive PivotTable on a Web or intranet site that lets users explore data relationships using their browsers.

PivotTable report An Excel feature that allows you to summarize worksheet data in the form of a table in which you can rearrange, or "pivot," parts of the table structure to explore new data relationships; also called a PivotTable.

PivotTable toolbar Contains buttons that allow you to manipulate data in a PivotTable.

Plot area The area of a chart that contains the chart itself, its axes, and the legend.

Point A unit of measure used for fonts and row height. One inch equals 72 points, or a point is equal to ½ of an inch.

Pointing method Specifying formula cell references by selecting the desired cell with the mouse instead of typing its cell reference; it eliminates typing errors. Also known as Pointing.

Populate a worksheet with XML data The process of importing an XML file and filling the mapped elements on the worksheet with data from the XML file.

Portrait orientation A print setting that positions the worksheet on the page so the page is taller than it is wide.

Post To place an interactive workbook in a shared location.

Precedents In formula auditing, the cells that are used in the formula to calculate the value of a given cell.

Presentation graphics program A program such as Microsoft PowerPoint that you can use to create slide show presentations.

Preview A view of the worksheet exactly as it will appear on paper.

Primary Key The field in a database that contains unique information for each record.

Print area A portion of a worksheet that you can define using the Print Area command on the File menu; after you define a print area, clicking the Print icon on the Standard toolbar prints only that worksheet area.

Print title In a list that spans more than one page, the field names that print at the top of every printed page.

Procedure A sequence of Visual Basic statements contained in a macro that accomplishes a specific task.

Procedure footer In Visual Basic, the last line of a Sub procedure.

Procedure header The first line in a Visual Basic procedure.

Program Task-oriented software (such as Excel or Word) that enables you to perform a certain type of task, such as data calculation or word processing.

Program code Macro instructions, written in the Visual Basic for Applications programming language.

Project In the Visual Basic Editor, the equivalent of a workbook; a project contains Visual Basic modules.

Project Explorer In the Visual Basic Editor, a window that lists all open projects (or workbooks) and the worksheets and modules they contain.

Property In Visual Basic, an attribute of an object that describes its character or behavior.

Properties window In the Visual Basic Editor, the window that displays a list of characteristics, or properties, associated with a module.

Publish To place an Excel workbook or worksheet on a Web site or an intranet in HTML format so that others can access it using their Web browsers.

Range A selected group of adjacent cells.

Range finder A feature that outlines an equation's arguments in blue and green.

Range object In Visual Basic, an object that represents a cell or a range of cells.

Record In a list (an Excel database), data about an object or a person.

Refresh To update a PivotTable so it reflects changes to the underlying data.

Relative cell reference A type of cell reference used to indicate a relative position in the worksheet. It allows you to copy and move formulas from one area to another of the same dimensions. Excel automatically changes the column and row numbers to reflect the new position. Also known as Relative reference.

Research services Reference information available through the Research task pane that can be inserted into your document.

Retrieve In Autofilter, to search for and list records.

Route To send an e-mail attachment sequentially to each user in a list, who then forwards it to the next user on the list.

Routing slip A list of e-mail users who are to receive an e-mail attachment.

Row height The vertical dimension of a cell.

Row heading The gray box containing the row number to the left of the row.

Run To play, as a macro.

Scenario A set of values you use to forecast results; the Excel Scenario Manager lets you store and manage different scenarios.

Scenario summary An Excel table that compiles data from various scenarios so that you can view the scenario results next to each other for easy comparison.

Schema In an XML document, a list of the fields, called elements or attributes, and their characteristics.

Search criterion The specification for data that you want to find in an Excel list, such as "Brisbane" or "is greater than 1000."

Series of labels Preprogrammed series, such as days of the week and months of the year. They are formed by typing the first word of the series, then dragging the fill handle to select and fill the desired range of cells.

Shared workbook An Excel workbook that several users can open and modify.

Sheet A term used for a worksheet.

Sheet tab A description at the bottom of each worksheet that identifies it in a workbook. In an open workbook, move to a worksheet by clicking its sheet tab. Also known as Worksheet tab.

Sheet tab scrolling buttons Buttons that enable you to move among sheets within a workbook.

Single-file Web page A Web page that integrates all of the worksheets and graphical elements from a workbook into a single file in the MHTML file format, making it easier to publish to the Web. Users who have IE 4.0 or higher can open a Web page saved in MHTML format.

Sizing handles Small boxes appearing along the corners and sides of charts and graphic images that are used for moving and resizing.

Sort To change the order of records in a list according to one or more fields, such as Last Name.

Sort keys Criteria on which a sort, or a reordering of data, is based.

Source list The list on which a PivotTable is based.

Source program In a data exchange, the program used to create the data you are embedding or linking.

Standard chart type A commonly used column, bar, pie, or area chart in the Excel program; each type has several variations. For example, a column chart variation is the Columns with Depth.

Standard toolbar A toolbar that contains buttons for frequently used operating and editing commands.

Statement In Visual Basic, a line of code.

Status bar The bar at the bottom of the Excel window that provides information about various keys, commands, and processes.

Style A named combination of formatting characteristics, such as bold, italic, and zero decimal places.

Sub procedure A series of Visual Basic statements that performs an action but does not return a value.

SUM The most frequently used function, this adds columns or rows of cells.

Summary function In a PivotTable, a function that determines the type of calculation applied to the PivotTable data, such as SUM or COUNT.

Syntax In the Visual Basic programming language, the formatting rules that must be followed so that the macro will run correctly.

Table In an Access database, a list of data. In Excel, a special list containing worksheet data that can be searched using Excel features.

Target The location that a hyperlink displays after you click it.

Target cell In what-if analysis (specifically, in Excel Solver), the cell containing the formula.

Task pane A window area to the right of the worksheet that provides worksheet options, such as creating a new workbook, conducting a search, inserting Clip Art, and using the Office Clipboard.

Task pane list arrow Lets you switch between 11 different task panes.

Template A workbook containing text, formulas, macros, and formatting you use repeatedly; when you create a new document, you can open a document based on the template workbook. The new document will automatically contain the formatting, text, formulas, and macros in the template.

Text annotations Labels added to a chart to draw attention to a particular area.

Text color The color applied to text in a cell or on a chart.

Text file A file that consists of text but no formatting. It is also called an ASCII file.

Tick marks Notations of a scale of measure on a chart axis.

Title bar The bar at the top of the program window that indicates the program name and the name of the current file.

Toggle button A button that turns a feature on and off.

Toolbar A bar that contains buttons that you can click to perform commands.

Toolbar Options button A button you click on a toolbar to view toolbar buttons not currently visible.

Tracers In Excel worksheet auditing, arrows that point from cells that might have caused an error to the active cell containing an error.

Track To identify and keep a record of who makes which changes to a workbook.

Trendline A chart that represents trends in a data series.

Truncate To shorten the display of cell information because a cell is too wide.

Two-input data table A range of cells that shows resulting values when two input values in a formula are changed.

Type a question for help box Area on the menu bar in which you can query the Excel help system by typing a question.

URL *See* Uniform Resource Locator.

Uniform Resource Locator (URL) A unique Web address that identifies a Web page.

Validation *See* Data Validation.

Validation Circles In formula auditing, the circles that identify invalid data.

Value A number, formula, or function used in calculations.

Value axis Also known as the y-axis in a 2-dimensional chart, this area often contains numerical values that help you interpret the size of chart elements. In a 3-dimensional chart, the z-axis.

Variable In the Visual Basic programming language, an area in memory in which you can temporarily store an item of information; variables are often declared in Dim statements such as *DimNameAsString*.

View A set of display or print settings that you can name and save for access at another time. You can save multiple views of a worksheet.

Virus Destructive software that can damage your computer files.

Visual Basic Editor A program that lets you display and edit macro code.

Visual Basic for Applications (VBA) A programming language used to create macros in Excel.

Web discussion Comments attached to an Excel worksheet that you will save as an HTML document, allowing people viewing your worksheet on the Web to review and reply to your comments.

Web query An Excel feature that lets you obtain data from a Web, Internet, or intranet site and places it in an Excel workbook for analysis.

What-if analysis A decision-making feature in which data is changed and formulas based on it are automatically recalculated.

Wildcard A special symbol you use in defining search criteria in the data form or Replace dialog box. The most common types of wildcards are the question mark (?), which stands for any single character, and the asterisk (*), which represents any group of characters.

Window A rectangular area of a screen where you view and work on the open file.

WordArt Specially formatted text, created using the WordArt button on the Drawing toolbar.

Workbook A collection of related worksheets contained within a single file.

Worksheet An electronic spreadsheet containing 256 columns by 65,536 rows.

Worksheet tab *See* Sheet tab.

Worksheet window Includes the tools that enable you to create and work with worksheets.

Workspace An Excel file with an .xlw extension containing information about the identity, view, and placement of a set of open workbooks. Instead of opening each workbook individually, you can open the workspace file instead.

X-axis The horizontal axis in a chart; because it often shows data categories, such as months, it is also called the category axis.

X-axis label A label describing a chart's x-axis.

XML (Extensible Markup Language) A system for defining languages using tags to structure data.

XY (scatter) chart Compares trends over uneven time or measurement intervals; used in scientific and engineering disciplines for trend spotting and extrapolation.

Y-axis The vertical axis in a chart; because it often shows numerical values in a 2-dimensional chart, it is also called the value axis.

Y-axis label A label describing the y-axis of a chart.

Zoom A feature that enables you to focus on a larger or smaller part of the worksheet in Print Preview.

Index